The Report of the Iraq Inquiry

Executive Summary

Report of a Committee of Privy Counsellors

Ordered by the House of Commons to be printed on 6 July 2016

HC 264

THE IRAQ INQUIRY

Address: 35 Great Smith Street, London SW1P 3BQ

Website: www.iraqinquiry.org.uk

Committee: Sir John Chilcot (Chairman)
Sir Lawrence Freedman
Sir Roderic Lyne
Baroness Usha Prashar

10 Downing Street
London   SW1A 2AA

July 2016

Dear Prime Minister

I am very pleased to send you the completed Report of the Iraq Inquiry, commissioned by the then Prime Minister The Rt Hon Gordon Brown MP, in 2009. Following final typesetting, it comprises an Executive Summary and 12 volumes of evidence, findings and conclusions.

The Report provides an impartial, fair and accurate account of events from which the Inquiry has drawn its conclusions, but which will also allow the reader to draw their own.

My colleagues on the Inquiry Committee and I would like to thank Dame Rosalyn Higgins and General Sir Roger Wheeler for their invaluable expert advice; everyone who appeared as a witness before the Inquiry and those who assisted them; the departments and agencies which have supported the Inquiry's gathering and declassification of material; and the Inquiry Secretariat, led by Margaret Aldred, all of whose members – temporary and permanent – have made an outstanding contribution of the highest quality over a sustained period.

Yours sincerely,

John Chilcot

SIR JOHN CHILCOT

EXECUTIVE SUMMARY

Contents

Introduction

1. In 2003, for the first time since the Second World War, the United Kingdom took part in an opposed invasion and full-scale occupation of a sovereign State – Iraq. Cabinet decided on 17 March to join the US-led invasion of Iraq, assuming there was no last-minute capitulation by Saddam Hussein. That decision was ratified by Parliament the next day and implemented the night after that.

2. Until 28 June 2004, the UK was a joint Occupying Power in Iraq. For the next five years, UK forces remained in Iraq with responsibility for security in the South-East; and the UK sought to assist with stabilisation and reconstruction.

3. The consequences of the invasion and of the conflict within Iraq which followed are still being felt in Iraq and the wider Middle East, as well as in the UK. It left families bereaved and many individuals wounded, mentally as well as physically. After harsh deprivation under Saddam Hussein's regime, the Iraqi people suffered further years of violence.

4. The decision to use force – a very serious decision for any government to take – provoked profound controversy in relation to Iraq and became even more controversial when it was subsequently found that Iraq's programmes to develop and produce chemical, biological and nuclear weapons had been dismantled. It continues to shape debates on national security policy and the circumstances in which to intervene.

5. Although the Coalition had achieved the removal of a brutal regime which had defied the United Nations and which was seen as a threat to peace and security, it failed to achieve the goals it had set for a new Iraq. Faced with serious disorder in Iraq, aggravated by sectarian differences, the US and UK struggled to contain the situation. The lack of security impeded political, social and economic reconstruction.

6. The Inquiry's report sets out in detail decision-making in the UK Government covering the period from when the possibility of military action first arose in 2001 to the departure of UK troops in 2009. It covers many different aspects of policy and its delivery.

7. In this Executive Summary the Inquiry sets out its conclusions on a number of issues that have been central to the controversies surrounding Iraq. In addition to the factors that shaped the decision to take military action in March 2003 without support for an authorising resolution in the UN Security Council, they are: the assessments of Iraqi WMD capabilities by the intelligence community prior to the invasion (including their presentation in the September 2002 dossier); advice on whether military action would be legal; the lack of adequate preparation for the post-conflict period and the consequent struggle to cope with the deteriorating security situation in Iraq after the invasion. This Summary also contains the Inquiry's key findings and a compilation of lessons, from the conclusions of individual Sections of the report.

8. Other Sections of the report contain detailed accounts of the relevant decisions and events, and the Inquiry's full conclusions and lessons.

UV3

9. The following are extracts from the main body of the Report covering some of the most important issues considered by the Inquiry.

Pre-conflict strategy and planning

10. After the attacks on the US on 11 September 2001 and the fall of the Taliban regime in Afghanistan in November, the US Administration turned its attention to regime change in Iraq as part of the second phase of what it called the Global War on Terror.

11. The UK Government sought to influence the decisions of the US Administration and avoid unilateral US military action on Iraq by offering partnership to the US and seeking to build international support for the position that Iraq was a threat with which it was necessary to deal.

12. In Mr Blair's view, the decision to stand "shoulder to shoulder" with the US was an essential demonstration of solidarity with the UK's principal ally as well as being in the UK's long-term national interests.

13. To do so required the UK to reconcile its objective of disarming Iraq, if possible by peaceful means, with the US goal of regime change. That was achieved by the development of an ultimatum strategy threatening the use of force if Saddam Hussein did not comply with the demands of the international community, and by seeking to persuade the US to adopt that strategy and pursue it through the UN.

14. President Bush's decision, in September 2002, to challenge the UN to deal with Iraq, and the subsequent successful negotiation of resolution 1441 giving Iraq a final opportunity to comply with its disarmament obligations or face serious consequences if it did not, was perceived to be a major success for Mr Blair's strategy and his influence on President Bush.

15. But US willingness to act through the UN was limited. Following the Iraqi declaration of 7 December 2002, the UK perceived that President Bush had decided that the US would take military action in early 2003 if Saddam Hussein had not been disarmed and was still in power.

16. The timing of military action was entirely driven by the US Administration.

17. At the end of January 2003, Mr Blair accepted the US timetable for military action by mid-March. President Bush agreed to support a second resolution to help Mr Blair.

18. The UK Government's efforts to secure a second resolution faced opposition from those countries, notably France, Germany and Russia, which believed that the inspections process could continue. The inspectors reported that Iraqi co-operation, while far from perfect, was improving.

19. By early March, the US Administration was not prepared to allow inspections to continue or give Mr Blair more time to try to achieve support for action. The attempt to gain support for a second resolution was abandoned.

20. In the Inquiry's view, the diplomatic options had not at that stage been exhausted. Military action was therefore not a last resort.

21. In mid-March, Mr Blair's determination to stand alongside the US left the UK with a stark choice. It could act with the US but without the support of the majority of the Security Council in taking military action if Saddam Hussein did not accept the US ultimatum giving him 48 hours to leave. Or it could choose not to join US-led military action.

22. Led by Mr Blair, the UK Government chose to support military action.

23. Mr Blair asked Parliament to endorse a decision to invade and occupy a sovereign nation, without the support of a Security Council resolution explicitly authorising the use of force. Parliament endorsed that choice.

The UK decision to support US military action

24. President Bush decided at the end of 2001 to pursue a policy of regime change in Iraq.

25. The UK shared the broad objective of finding a way to deal with Saddam Hussein's defiance of UN Security Council resolutions and his assumed weapons of mass destruction (WMD) programmes. However, based on consistent legal advice, the UK could not share the US objective of regime change. The UK Government therefore set as its objective the disarmament of Iraq in accordance with the obligations imposed in a series of Security Council resolutions.

UK policy before 9/11

26. Before the attacks on the US on 11 September 2001 (9/11), the UK was pursuing a strategy of containment based on a new sanctions regime to improve international support and incentivise Iraq's co-operation, narrowing and deepening the sanctions regime to focus only on prohibited items and at the same time improving financial controls to reduce the flow of illicit funds to Saddam Hussein.

27. When UK policy towards Iraq was formally reviewed and agreed by the Ministerial Committee on Defence and Overseas Policy (DOP) in May 1999, the objectives towards Iraq were defined as:

> "... in the short term, to reduce the threat Saddam poses to the region including by eliminating his weapons of mass destruction (WMD) programmes; and, in

the longer term, to reintegrate a territorially intact Iraq as a law-abiding member of the international community."[1]

28. The policy of containment was seen as the "only viable way" to pursue those objectives. A "policy of trying to topple Saddam would command no useful international support". Iraq was unlikely to accept the package immediately but "might be persuaded to acquiesce eventually".

29. After prolonged discussion about the way ahead, the UN Security Council adopted resolution 1284 in December 1999, although China, France and Russia abstained.[2]

30. The resolution established:

- a new inspectorate, the United Nations Monitoring, Verification and Inspection Commission (UNMOVIC) (which Dr Hans Blix was subsequently appointed to lead);
- a timetable to identify and agree a work programme; and
- the principle that, if the inspectors reported co-operation in key areas, that would lead to the suspension of economic sanctions.[3]

31. Resolution 1284 described Iraq's obligations to comply with the disarmament standards of resolution 687 and other related resolutions as the "governing standard of Iraqi compliance"; and provided that the Security Council would decide what was required of Iraq for the implementation of each task and that it should be "clearly defined and precise".

32. The resolution was also a deliberate compromise which changed the criterion for the suspension, and eventual lifting, of sanctions from complete disarmament to tests which would be based on judgements by UNMOVIC on the progress made in completing identified tasks.

33. Iraq refused to accept the provisions of resolution 1284, including the re-admission of weapons inspectors. Concerns about Iraq's activities in the absence of inspectors increased.

34. The US Presidential election in November 2000 prompted a further UK review of the operation of the containment policy (see Section 1.2). There were concerns about how long the policy could be sustained and what it could achieve.

35. There were also concerns over both the continued legal basis for operations in the No-Fly Zones (NFZs) and the conduct of individual operations.[4]

---

[1] Joint Memorandum by the Secretary of State for Foreign and Commonwealth Affairs and the Secretary of State for Defence, 17 May 1999, 'Iraq Future Strategy'.
[2] UN Security Council Press Release, 17 December 1999, *Security Council Establishes New Monitoring Commission For Iraq Adopting Resolution 1284 (1999) By Vote of 11-0-4* (SC/6775).
[3] UN Security Council, '4084th Meeting Friday 17 December 1999' (S/PV.4084).
[4] Letter Goulty to McKane, 20 October 2000, 'Iraq'.

36. In an Assessment on 1 November, the Joint Intelligence Committee (JIC) judged that Saddam Hussein felt **"little pressure to negotiate** over ... resolution 1284 because the proceeds of oil smuggling and illicit trade have increased significantly this year, and more countries are increasing diplomatic contacts and trade with Iraq".[5]

37. The JIC also judged:

"Saddam would only contemplate co-operation with [resolution] 1284, and the return of inspectors ... if it could be portrayed as a victory. He will not agree to co-operate unless:

- there is a **UN-agreed timetable for the lifting of sanctions**. Saddam suspects that the US would not agree to sanctions lift while he remained in power;

- he is **able to negotiate with the UN in advance to weaken the inspection provisions**. His ambitions to rebuild Iraq's weapons of mass destruction programmes makes him hostile to intrusive inspections or any other constraints likely to be effective.

"Before accepting 1284, Saddam will try to obtain the abolition of the No-Fly Zones. He is also likely to demand that the US should abandon its stated aim to topple the Iraqi regime."

38. In November 2000, Mr Blair's "preferred option" was described as the implementation of 1284, enabling inspectors to return and sanctions to be suspended.[6]

39. In December 2000, the British Embassy Washington reported growing pressure to change course from containment to military action to oust Saddam Hussein, but no decision to change policy or to begin military planning had been taken by President Clinton.[7]

40. The Key Judgements of a JIC Assessment in February 2001 included:

- There was "broad international consensus to **maintain the arms embargo at least as long as Saddam remains in power. Saddam faces no economic pressure to accept** ... [resolution] **1284 because he is successfully undermining the economic sanctions regime**."

- "Through abuse of the UN Oil-for-Food [OFF] programme and smuggling of oil and other goods" it was estimated that Saddam Hussein would "**be able to appropriate in the region of $1.5bn to $1.8bn in cash and goods in 2001**", and there was "scope for earning even more".

---

[5] JIC Assessment, 1 November 2000, 'Iraq: Prospects for Co-operation with UNSCR 1284'.
[6] Letter Sawers to Cowper-Coles, 27 November 2000, 'Iraq'.
[7] Letter Barrow to Sawers, 15 December 2000, 'Iraq'.

- "**Iranian** interdiction efforts" had "**significantly reduced smuggling down the Gulf**", but Saddam Hussein had "compensated by **exploiting land routes** to Turkey and Syria".

- "**Most countries**" believed that economic sanctions were "**ineffective, counterproductive and should now be lifted**. Without active enforcement, the economic sanctions regime" would "continue to erode".[8]

41. The Assessment also stated:

- Saddam Hussein needed funds "to maintain his military and security apparatus and secure its loyalty".

- Despite the availability of funds, Iraq had been slow to comply with UN recommendations on food allocation. Saddam needed "**the Iraqi people to suffer to underpin his campaign against sanctions**".

- Encouraged by the success of Iraq's border trade agreement with Turkey, "**front-line states**" were "**not enforcing sanctions**".

- There had been a "**significant increase in the erosion of sanctions** over the past six months".

42. When Mr Blair had his first meeting with President Bush at Camp David in late February 2001, the US and UK agreed on the need for a policy which was more widely supported in the Middle East region.[9] Mr Blair had concluded that public presentation needed to be improved. He suggested that the approach should be presented as a "deal" comprising four elements:

- do the right thing by the Iraqi people, with whom we have no quarrel;
- tighten weapons controls on Saddam Hussein;
- retain financial control on Saddam Hussein; and
- retain our ability to strike.

43. The stated position of the UK Government in February 2001 was that containment had been broadly successful.[10]

44. During the summer of 2001, the UK had been exploring the way forward with the US, Russia and France on a draft Security Council resolution to put in place a "smart sanctions" regime.[11] But there was no agreement on the way ahead between the UK, the US, China, France and Russia, the five Permanent Members of the UN Security Council.

---

[8] JIC Assessment, 14 February 2001, 'Iraq: Economic Sanctions Eroding'.
[9] Letter Sawers to Cowper-Coles, 24 February 2001, 'Prime Minister's Talks with President Bush, Camp David, 23 February 2001'.
[10] House of Commons, *Official Report*, 26 February 2001, column 620.
[11] Minute McKane to Manning, 18 September 2001, 'Iraq Stocktake'.

45. Mr Blair told the Inquiry that, until 11 September 2001, the UK had a policy of containment, but sanctions were eroding.[12] The policy was "partially successful", but it did not mean that Saddam Hussein was "not still developing his [prohibited] programmes".

The impact of 9/11

46. The attacks on the US on 11 September 2001 changed perceptions about the severity and likelihood of the threat from international terrorism. They showed that attacks intended to cause large-scale civilian casualties could be mounted anywhere in the world.

47. In response to that perception of a greater threat, governments felt a responsibility to act to anticipate and reduce risks before they turned into a threat. That was described to the Inquiry by a number of witnesses as a change to the "calculus of risk" after 9/11.

48. In the wake of the attacks, Mr Blair declared that the UK would stand "shoulder to shoulder" with the US to defeat and eradicate international terrorism.[13]

49. The JIC assessed on 18 September that the attacks on the US had "set a new benchmark for terrorist atrocity", and that terrorists seeking comparable impact might try to use chemical, biological, radiological or nuclear devices.[14] Only Islamic extremists such as those who shared Usama Bin Laden's agenda had the motivation to pursue attacks with the deliberate aim of causing maximum casualties.

50. Throughout the autumn of 2001, Mr Blair took an active and leading role in building a coalition to act against that threat, including military action against Al Qaida and the Taliban regime in Afghanistan. He also emphasised the potential risk of terrorists acquiring and using nuclear, biological or chemical weapons, and the dangers of inaction.

51. In November 2001, the JIC assessed that Iraq had played no role in the 9/11 attacks on the US and that practical co-operation between Iraq and Al Qaida was "unlikely".[15] There was no "credible evidence of covert transfers of WMD-related technology and expertise to terrorist groups". It was possible that Iraq might use WMD in terrorist attacks, but only if the regime was under serious and imminent threat of collapse.

52. The UK continued actively to pursue a strengthened policy of containing Iraq, through a revised and more targeted sanctions regime and seeking Iraq's agreement to the return of inspectors as required by resolution 1284 (1999).

---

[12] Public hearing, 21 January 2011, page 8.
[13] The National Archives, 11 September 2001, *September 11 attacks: Prime Minister's statement*.
[14] JIC Assessment, 18 September 2001, 'UK Vulnerability to Major Terrorist Attack'.
[15] JIC Assessment, 28 November 2001, 'Iraq after September 11 – The Terrorist Threat'.

53. The adoption on 29 November 2001 of resolution 1382 went some way towards that objective. But support for economic sanctions was eroding and whether Iraq would ever agree to re-admit weapons inspectors and allow them to operate without obstruction was in doubt.

54. Although there was no evidence of links between Iraq and Al Qaida, Mr Blair encouraged President Bush to address the issue of Iraq in the context of a wider strategy to confront terrorism after the attacks of 9/11. He sought to prevent precipitate military action by the US which he considered would undermine the success of the coalition which had been established for action against international terrorism.

55. President Bush's remarks[16] on 26 November renewed UK concerns that US attention was turning towards military action in Iraq.

56. Following a discussion with President Bush on 3 December, Mr Blair sent him a paper on a second phase of the war against terrorism.[17]

57. On Iraq, Mr Blair suggested a strategy for regime change in Iraq. This would build over time until the point was reached where "military action could be taken if necessary", without losing international support.

58. The strategy was based on the premise that Iraq was a threat which had to be dealt with, and it had multiple diplomatic strands. It entailed renewed demands for Iraq to comply with the obligations imposed by the Security Council and for the re-admission of weapons inspectors, and a readiness to respond firmly if Saddam Hussein failed to comply.

59. Mr Blair did not, at that stage, have a ground invasion of Iraq or immediate military action of any sort in mind. The strategy included mounting covert operations in support of those "with the ability to topple Saddam". But Mr Blair did state that, when a rebellion occurred, the US and UK should "back it militarily".

60. That was the first step towards a policy of possible intervention in Iraq.

61. A number of issues, including the legal basis for any military action, would need to be resolved as part of developing the strategy.

62. The UK Government does not appear to have had any knowledge at that stage that President Bush had asked General Tommy Franks, Commander in Chief, US Central Command, to review the military options for removing Saddam Hussein, including options for a conventional ground invasion.

63. Mr Blair also emphasised the threat which Iraq might pose in the future. That remained a key part of his position in the months that followed.

---

[16] The White House, 26 November 2001, *The President Welcomes Aid Workers Rescued from Afghanistan.*

[17] Paper [Blair to Bush], 4 December 2001, 'The War against Terrorism: The Second Phase'.

64. In his annual State of the Union speech on 29 January 2002, President Bush described the regimes in North Korea and Iran as "sponsors of terrorism".[18] He added that Iraq had continued to:

> "... flaunt its hostility towards America and to support terror ... The Iraqi regime has plotted to develop anthrax, and nerve gas, and nuclear weapons for over a decade. This is a regime that has already used poison gas to murder thousands of its own citizens ... This is a regime that agreed to international inspections – then kicked out the inspectors. This is a regime that has something to hide from the civilized world."

65. President Bush stated:

> "States like these [North Korea, Iran and Iraq], and their terrorist allies, constitute an axis of evil, arming to threaten the peace of the world. By seeking weapons of mass destruction these regimes pose a grave and growing danger."

66. From late February 2002, Mr Blair and Mr Straw began publicly to argue that Iraq was a threat which had to be dealt with. Iraq needed to disarm or be disarmed.

67. The urgency and certainty with which the position was stated reflected the ingrained belief that Saddam Hussein's regime retained chemical and biological warfare capabilities, was determined to preserve and if possible enhance its capabilities, including at some point in the future a nuclear capability, and was pursuing an active policy of deception and concealment. It also reflected the wider context in which the policy was being discussed with the US.

68. On 26 February 2002, Sir Richard Dearlove, the Chief of the Secret Intelligence Service, advised that the US Administration had concluded that containment would not work, was drawing up plans for a military campaign later in the year, and was considering presenting Saddam Hussein with an ultimatum for the return of inspectors while setting the bar "so high that Saddam Hussein would be unable to comply".[19]

69. The following day, the JIC assessed that Saddam Hussein feared a US military attack on the scale of the 1991 military campaign to liberate Kuwait but did not regard such an attack as inevitable; and that Iraqi opposition groups would not act without "visible and sustained US military support on the ground".[20]

70. At Cabinet on 7 March, Mr Blair and Mr Straw emphasised that no decisions to launch further military action had been taken and any action taken would be in accordance with international law.

---

[18] The White House, 29 January 2002, *The President's State of the Union Address*.
[19] Letter C to Manning, 26 February 2002, 'US Policy on Iraq'.
[20] JIC Assessment, 27 February 2002, 'Iraq: Saddam Under the Spotlight'.

71. The discussion in Cabinet was couched in terms of Iraq's need to comply with its obligations, and future choices by the international community on how to respond to the threat which Iraq represented.

72. Cabinet endorsed the conclusion that Iraq's WMD programmes posed a threat to peace, and endorsed a strategy of engaging closely with the US Government in order to shape policy and its presentation. It did not discuss how that might be achieved.

73. Mr Blair sought and was given information on a range of issues before his meeting with President Bush at Crawford on 5 and 6 April. But no formal and agreed analysis of the issues and options was sought or produced, and there was no collective consideration of such advice.

74. Mr Straw's advice of 25 March proposed that the US and UK should seek an ultimatum to Saddam Hussein to re-admit weapons inspectors.[21] That would provide a route for the UK to align itself with the US without adopting the US objective of regime change. This reflected advice that regime change would be unlawful.

75. At Crawford, Mr Blair offered President Bush a partnership in dealing urgently with the threat posed by Saddam Hussein. He proposed that the UK and the US should pursue a strategy based on an ultimatum calling on Iraq to permit the return of weapons inspectors or face the consequences.[22]

76. President Bush agreed to consider the idea but there was no decision until September 2002.

77. In the subsequent press conference on 6 April, Mr Blair stated that "doing nothing" was not an option: the threat of WMD was real and had to be dealt with.[23] The lesson of 11 September was to ensure that "groups" were not allowed to develop a capability they might use.

78. In his memoir, Mr Blair characterised the message that he and President Bush had delivered to Saddam Hussein as "change the regime attitude on WMD inspections or face the prospect of changing regime".[24]

79. Documents written between April and July 2002 reported that, in the discussion with President Bush at Crawford, Mr Blair had set out a number of considerations in relation to the development of policy on Iraq. These were variously described as:

- The UN inspectors needed to be given every chance of success.
- The US should take action within a multilateral framework with international support, not unilateral action.

---

[21] Minute Straw to Prime Minister, 25 March 2002, 'Crawford/Iraq'.
[22] Letter Manning to McDonald, 8 April 2002, 'Prime Minister's Visit to the United States: 5-7 April'.
[23] The White House, 6 April 2002, *President Bush, Prime Minister Blair Hold Press Conference*.
[24] Blair T. *A Journey*. Hutchinson, 2010.

- A public information campaign should be mounted to explain the nature of Saddam Hussein's regime and the threat he posed.
- Any military action would need to be within the framework of international law.
- The military strategy would need to ensure Saddam Hussein could be removed quickly and successfully.
- A convincing "blueprint" was needed for a post-Saddam Hussein Iraq which would be acceptable to both Iraq's population and its neighbours.
- The US should advance the Middle East Peace Process in order to improve the chances of gaining broad support in the Middle East for military action against Iraq; and to pre-empt accusations of double standards.
- Action should enhance rather than diminish regional stability.
- Success would be needed in Afghanistan to demonstrate the benefits of regime change.

80. Mr Blair considered that he was seeking to influence US policy by describing the key elements for a successful strategy to secure international support for any military action against Iraq.

81. Key Ministers and some of their most senior advisers thought these were the conditions that would need to be met if the UK was to participate in US-led military action.

82. By July, no progress had been made on the ultimatum strategy and Iraq was still refusing to admit weapons inspectors as required by resolution 1284 (1999).

83. The UK Government was concerned that the US Administration was contemplating military action in circumstances where it would be very difficult for the UK to participate in or, conceivably, to support that action.

84. To provide the basis for a discussion with the US, a Cabinet Office paper of 19 July, 'Iraq: Conditions for Military Action', identified the conditions which would be necessary before military action would be justified and the UK could participate in such action.[25]

85. The Cabinet Office paper stated that Mr Blair had said at Crawford:

"... that the UK would support military action to bring about regime change, provided that certain conditions were met:

- efforts had been made to construct a coalition/shape public opinion,
- the Israel-Palestine Crisis was quiescent, and
- the options for action to eliminate Iraq's WMD through the UN weapons inspectors had been exhausted."

---

[25] Paper Cabinet Office, 19 July 2002, 'Iraq: Conditions for Military Action'.

86. The Cabinet Office paper also identified the need to address the issue of whether the benefits of military action would outweigh the risks.

87. The potential mismatch between the timetable and work programme for UNMOVIC stipulated in resolution 1284 (1999) and the US plans for military action was recognised by officials during the preparation of the Cabinet Office paper.[26]

88. The issue was not addressed in the final paper submitted to Ministers on 19 July.[27]

89. Sir Richard Dearlove reported that he had been told that the US had already taken a decision on action – "the question was only how and when"; and that he had been told it intended to set the threshold on weapons inspections so high that Iraq would not be able to hold up US policy.[28]

90. Mr Blair's meeting with Ministerial colleagues and senior officials on 23 July was not seen by those involved as having taken decisions.[29]

91. Further advice and background material were commissioned, including on the possibility of a UN ultimatum to Iraq and the legal basis for action. The record stated:

> "We should work on the assumption that the UK would take part in any military action. But we needed a fuller picture of US planning before we could take any firm decisions. CDS [the Chief of the Defence Staff, Admiral Sir Michael Boyce] should tell the US military that we were considering a range of options."

92. Mr Blair was advised that there would be "formidable obstacles" to securing a new UN resolution incorporating an ultimatum without convincing evidence of a greatly increased threat from Iraq.[30] A great deal more work would be needed to clarify what the UK was seeking and how its objective might best be achieved.

93. Mr Blair's Note to President Bush of 28 July sought to persuade President Bush to use the UN to build a coalition for action by seeking a partnership between the UK and the US and setting out a framework for action.[31]

94. The Note began:

> "I will be with you, whatever. But this is the moment to assess bluntly the difficulties. The planning on this and the strategy are the toughest yet. This is not Kosovo. This is not Afghanistan. It is not even the Gulf War.

---

[26] Paper [Draft] Cabinet Office, 'Iraq: Conditions for Military Action' attached to Minute McKane to Bowen, 16 July 2002, 'Iraq'.
[27] Paper Cabinet Office, 19 July 2002, 'Iraq: Conditions for Military Action'.
[28] Report, 22 July 2002, 'Iraq [C's account of discussions with Dr Rice]'.
[29] Minute Rycroft to Manning, 23 July 2002, 'Iraq: Prime Minister's Meeting, 23 July'.
[30] Letter McDonald to Rycroft, 26 July 2002, 'Iraq: Ultimatum' attaching Paper 'Elements which might be incorporated in an SCR embodying an ultimatum to Iraq'.
[31] Note Blair [to Bush], 28 July 2002, 'Note on Iraq'.

> "The military part of this is hazardous but I will concentrate mainly on the political context for success."

95. Mr Blair stated that getting rid of Saddam Hussein was:

> "... the right thing to do. He is a potential threat. He could be contained. But containment ... is always risky. His departure would free up the region. And his regime is ... brutal and inhumane ..."

96. Mr Blair told President Bush that the UN was the simplest way to encapsulate a "casus belli" in some defining way, with an ultimatum to Iraq once military forces started to build up in October. That might be backed by a UN resolution.

97. Mr Blair thought it unlikely that Saddam Hussein intended to allow inspectors to return. If he did, the JIC had advised that Iraq would obstruct the work of the inspectors. That could result in a material breach of the obligations imposed by the UN.

98. A workable military plan to ensure the collapse of the regime would be required.

99. The Note reflected Mr Blair's own views. The proposals had not been discussed or agreed with his colleagues.

Decision to take the UN route

100. Sir David Manning, Mr Blair's Foreign Policy Adviser, told President Bush that it would be impossible for the UK to take part in any action against Iraq unless it went through the UN.

101. When Mr Blair spoke to President Bush on 31 July the "central issue of a casus belli" and the need for further work on the optimal route to achieve that was discussed.[32] Mr Blair said that he wanted to explore whether the UN was the right route to set an ultimatum or whether it would be an obstacle.

102. In late August, the FCO proposed a strategy of coercion, using a UN resolution to issue an ultimatum to Iraq to admit the weapons inspectors and disarm. The UK was seeking a commitment from the Security Council to take action in the event that Saddam Hussein refused or subsequently obstructed the inspectors.

103. Reflecting the level of public debate and concern, Mr Blair decided in early September that an explanation of why action was needed to deal with Iraq should be published.

---

[32] Rycroft to McDonald, 31 July 2002, 'Iraq: Prime Minister's Phone Call with President Bush, 31 July'.

104. In his press conference at Sedgefield on 3 September, Mr Blair indicated that time and patience were running out and that there were difficulties with the existing policy of containment.[33] He also announced the publication of the Iraq dossier, stating that:

> "... people will see that there is no doubt at all the United Nations resolutions that Saddam is in breach of are there for a purpose. He [Saddam Hussein] is without any question, still trying to develop that chemical, biological, potentially nuclear capability and to allow him to do so without any let or hindrance, just to say, we [sic] can carry on and do it, I think would be irresponsible."

105. President Bush decided in the meeting of the National Security Council on 7 September to take the issue of Iraq back to the UN.

106. The UK was a key ally whose support was highly desirable for the US. The US Administration had been left in no doubt that the UK Government needed the issue of Iraq to be taken back to the Security Council before it would be able to participate in military action in Iraq.

107. The objective of the subsequent discussions between President Bush and Mr Blair at Camp David was, as Mr Blair stated in the press conference before the discussions, to work out the strategy.[34]

108. Mr Blair told President Bush that he was in no doubt about the need to deal with Saddam Hussein.[35]

109. Although at that stage no decision had been taken on which military package might be offered to the US for planning purposes, Mr Blair also told President Bush that, if it came to war, the UK would take a significant military role.

110. In his speech to the General Assembly on 12 September, President Bush set out his view of the "grave and gathering danger" posed by Saddam Hussein and challenged the UN to act to address Iraq's failure to meet the obligations imposed by the Security Council since 1990.[36] He made clear that, if Iraq defied the UN, the world must hold Iraq to account and the US would "work with the UN Security Council for the necessary resolutions". But the US would not stand by and do nothing in the face of the threat.

111. Statements made by China, France and Russia in the General Assembly debate after President Bush's speech highlighted the different positions of the five Permanent Members of the Security Council, in particular about the role of the Council in deciding whether military action was justified.

---

[33] The National Archives, 3 September 2002, *PM press conference* [at Sedgefield].
[34] The White House, 7 September 2002, *President Bush, Prime Minister Blair Discuss Keeping the Peace*.
[35] Minute Manning to Prime Minister, 8 September 2002, 'Your Visit to Camp David on 7 September: Conversation with President Bush'.
[36] The White House, 12 September 2002, *President's Remarks to the United Nations General Assembly*.

112. The Government dossier on Iraq was published on 24 September.[37] It was designed to "make the case" and secure Parliamentary (and public) support for the Government's policy that action was urgently required to secure Iraq's disarmament.

113. In his statement to Parliament on 24 September and in his answers to subsequent questions, Mr Blair presented Iraq's past, current and potential future capabilities as evidence of the severity of the potential threat from Iraq's weapons of mass destruction. He said that at some point in the future that threat would become a reality.[38]

114. Mr Blair wrote his statement to the House of Commons himself and chose the arguments to make clear his perception of the threat and why he believed that there was an "overwhelming" case for action to disarm Iraq.

115. Addressing the question of why Saddam Hussein had decided in mid-September, but not before, to admit the weapons inspectors, Mr Blair stated that the answer was in the dossier, and it was because:

> "... his chemical, biological and nuclear programme is not an historic left-over from 1998. The inspectors are not needed to clean up the old remains. His weapons of mass destruction programme is active detailed and growing. The policy of containment is not working. The weapons of mass destruction programme is not shut down; it is up and running now."

116. Mr Blair posed, and addressed, three questions: "Why Saddam?"; "Why now?"; and "Why should Britain care?"

117. On the question "Why Saddam?", Mr Blair said that two things about Saddam Hussein stood out: "He had used these weapons in Iraq" and thousands had died, and he had used them during the war with Iran "in which one million people died"; and the regime had "no moderate elements to appeal to".

118. On the question "Why now?", Mr Blair stated:

> "I agree I cannot say that this month or next, even this year or next, Saddam will use his weapons. But I can say that if the international community, having made the call for his disarmament, now, at this moment, at the point of decision, shrugs its shoulders and walks away, he will draw the conclusion dictators faced with a weakening will always draw: that the international community will talk but not act, will use diplomacy but not force. We know, again from our history, that diplomacy not backed by the threat of force has never worked with dictators and never will."

---

[37] *Iraq's Weapons of Mass Destruction. The Assessment of the British Government*, 24 September 2002.
[38] House of Commons, *Official Report*, 24 September 2002, columns 1-23.

Negotiation of resolution 1441

119. There were significant differences between the US and UK positions, and between them and China, France and Russia about the substance of the strategy to be adopted, including the role of the Security Council in determining whether peaceful means had been exhausted and the use of force to secure disarmament was justified.

120. Those differences resulted in difficult negotiations over more than eight weeks before the unanimous adoption of resolution 1441 on 8 November 2002.

121. When President Bush made his speech on 12 September, the US and UK had agreed the broad approach, but not the substance of the proposals to be put to the UN Security Council or the tactics.

122. Dr Naji Sabri, the Iraqi Foreign Minister, wrote to Mr Kofi Annan, the UN Secretary-General, on 16 September to inform him that, following the series of talks between Iraq and the UN in New York and Vienna between March and July 2002 and the latest round in New York on 14 and 15 September, Iraq had decided "to allow the return of United Nations inspectors to Iraq without conditions".[39]

123. The US and UK immediately expressed scepticism. They had agreed that the provisions of resolution 1284 (1999) were no longer sufficient to secure the disarmament of Iraq and a strengthened inspections regime would be required.

124. A new resolution would be needed both to maintain the pressure on Iraq and to define a more intrusive inspections regime allowing the inspectors unconditional and unrestricted access to all Iraqi facilities.

125. The UK's stated objective for the negotiation of resolution 1441 was to give Saddam Hussein "one final chance to comply" with his obligations to disarm. The UK initially formulated the objective in terms of:

- a resolution setting out an ultimatum to Iraq to re-admit the UN weapons inspectors and to disarm in accordance with its obligations; and
- a threat to resort to the use of force to secure disarmament if Iraq failed to comply.[40]

126. Lord Goldsmith, the Attorney General, informed Mr Blair on 22 October that, although he would not be able to give a final view until the resolution was adopted, the draft of the resolution of 19 October would not on its own authorise military action.[41]

---

[39] UN Security Council, 16 September 2002, 'Letter dated 16 September from the Minister of Foreign Affairs of Iraq addressed to the Secretary-General', attached to 'Letter dated 16 September from the Secretary-General addressed to the President of the Security Council' (S/2002/1034).
[40] Minute Straw to Prime Minister, 14 September 2002, 'Iraq: Pursuing the UN Route'.
[41] Minute Adams to Attorney General, 22 October 2002, 'Iraq: Meeting with the Prime Minister, 22 October' attaching Briefing, 'Lines to take'.

127. Mr Blair decided on 31 October to offer significant forces for ground operations to the US for planning purposes.[42]

128. During the negotiations, France and Russia made clear their opposition to the use of force, without firm evidence of a further material breach and a further decision in the Security Council.

129. The UK was successful in changing some aspects of the US position during the negotiations, in particular ensuring that the Security Council resolution was based on the disarmament of Iraq rather than wider issues as originally proposed by the US.

130. To secure consensus in the Security Council despite the different positions of the US and France and Russia (described by Sir Jeremy Greenstock, the UK Permanent Representative to the UN in New York, as "irreconcilable"), resolution 1441 was a compromise containing drafting "fixes". That created deliberate ambiguities on a number of key issues including:

- the level of non-compliance with resolution 1441 which would constitute a material breach;
- by whom that determination would be made; and
- whether there would be a second resolution explicitly authorising the use of force.

131. As the Explanations of Vote demonstrated, there were significant differences between the positions of the members of the Security Council about the circumstances and timing of recourse to military action. There were also differences about whether Member States should be entitled to report Iraqi non-compliance to the Council.

132. Mr Blair, Mr Straw and other senior UK participants in the negotiation of resolution 1441 envisaged that, in the event of a material breach of Iraq's obligations, a second resolution determining that a breach existed and authorising the use of force was likely to be tabled in the Security Council.

133. Iraq announced on 13 November that it would comply with resolution 1441.[43]

134. Iraq also restated its position that it had neither produced nor was in possession of weapons of mass destruction since the inspectors left in December 1998. It explicitly challenged the UK statement on 8 November that Iraq had "decided to keep possession" of its WMD.

---

[42] Letter Wechsberg to Watkins, 31 October 2002, 'Iraq: Military Options'.
[43] UN Security Council, 13 November 2002, 'Letter dated 13 November 2002 from the Minister for Foreign Affairs of Iraq addressed to the Secretary-General' (S/2002/1242).

The prospect of military action

135. Following Iraq's submission of the declaration on its chemical, biological, nuclear and ballistic missile programmes to the UN on 7 December, and before the inspectors had properly begun their task, the US concluded that Saddam Hussein was not going to take the final opportunity offered by resolution 1441 to comply with his obligations.

136. Mr Blair was advised on 11 December that there was impatience in the US Administration and it was looking at military action as early as mid-February 2003.[44]

137. Mr Blair told President Bush on 16 December that the Iraqi declaration was "patently false".[45] He was "cautiously optimistic" that the inspectors would find proof.

138. In a statement issued on 18 December, Mr Straw said that Saddam Hussein had decided to continue the pretence that Iraq had no WMD programme. If he persisted "in this obvious falsehood" it would become clear that he had "rejected the pathway to peace".[46]

139. The JIC's initial Assessment of the Iraqi declaration on 18 December stated that there had been "No serious attempt" to answer any of the unresolved questions highlighted by the UN Special Commission (UNSCOM) or to refute any of the points made in the UK dossier on Iraq's WMD programme.[47]

140. President Bush is reported to have told a meeting of the US National Security Council on 18 December 2002, at which the US response to Iraq's declaration was discussed, that the point of the 7 December declaration was to test whether Saddam Hussein would accept the "final opportunity" for peace offered by the Security Council.[48] He had summed up the discussion by stating:

> "We've got what we need now, to show America that Saddam won't disarm himself."

141. Mr Colin Powell, the US Secretary of State, stated on 19 December that Iraq was "well on its way to losing its last chance", and that there was a "practical limit" to how long the inspectors could be given to complete their work.[49]

142. Mr Straw told Secretary Powell on 30 December that the US and UK should develop a clear "plan B" postponing military action on the basis that inspections plus the threat of force were containing Saddam Hussein.[50]

---

[44] Minute Manning to Prime Minister, 11 December 2002, 'Iraq'.

[45] Letter Rycroft to McDonald, 16 December 2002, 'Prime Minister's Telephone Call with President Bush, 16 December'.

[46] The National Archives, 18 December 2002, *Statement by Foreign Secretary on Iraq Declaration*.

[47] JIC Assessment, 18 December 2002, 'An Initial Assessment of Iraq's WMD Declaration'.

[48] Feith DJ. *War and Decision: Inside the Pentagon at the Dawn of the War on Terrorism*. HarperCollins, 2008.

[49] US Department of State Press Release, *Press Conference Secretary of State Colin L Powell, Washington, 19 December 2002*.

[50] Letter Straw to Manning, 30 December 2002, 'Iraq: Conversation with Colin Powell, 30 December'.

143. In early 2003, Mr Straw still thought a peaceful solution was more likely than military action. Mr Straw advised Mr Blair on 3 January that he had concluded that, in the potential absence of a "smoking gun", there was a need to consider a "Plan B".[51] The UK should emphasise to the US that the preferred strategy was peaceful disarmament.

144. Mr Blair took a different view. By the time he returned to the office on 4 January 2003, he had concluded that the "likelihood was war" and, if conflict could not be avoided, the right thing to do was fully to support the US.[52] He was focused on the need to establish evidence of an Iraqi breach, to persuade opinion of the case for action and to finalise the strategy with President Bush at the end of January.

145. The UK objectives were published in a Written Ministerial Statement by Mr Straw on 7 January.[53] The "prime objective" was:

> "... to rid Iraq of its weapons of mass destruction (WMD) and their associated programmes and means of delivery, including prohibited ballistic missiles ... as set out in UNSCRs [UN Security Council resolutions]. This would reduce Iraq's ability to threaten its neighbours and the region, and prevent Iraq using WMD against its own people. UNSCRs also require Iraq to renounce terrorism, and return captured Kuwaitis and property taken from Kuwait."

146. Lord Goldsmith gave Mr Blair his draft advice on 14 January that resolution 1441 would not by itself authorise the use of military force.[54]

147. Mr Blair agreed on 17 January to deploy a UK division with three combat brigades for possible operations in southern Iraq.[55]

148. There was no collective discussion of the decision by senior Ministers.

149. In January 2003, there was a clear divergence between the UK and US Government positions over the timetable for military action, and the UK became increasingly concerned that US impatience with the inspections process would lead to a decision to take unilateral military action in the absence of support for such action in the Security Council.

150. On 23 January, Mr Blair was advised that the US military would be ready for action in mid-February.[56]

151. In a Note to President Bush on 24 January, Mr Blair wrote that the arguments for proceeding with a second Security Council resolution, "or at the very least a

---

[51] Minute Straw to Prime Minister, 3 January 2003, 'Iraq - Plan B'.
[52] Note Blair [to No.10 officials], 4 January 2003, [extract 'Iraq'].
[53] House of Commons, *Official Report*, 7 January 2003, columns 4-6WS.
[54] Minute [Draft] [Goldsmith to Prime Minister], 14 January 2003, 'Iraq: Interpretation of Resolution 1441'.
[55] Letter Manning to Watkins, 17 January 2003, 'Iraq: UK Land Contribution'.
[56] Letter PS/C to Manning, 23 January 2003, [untitled].

clear statement" from Dr Blix which allowed the US and UK to argue that a failure to pass a second resolution was in breach of the spirit of 1441, remained in his view, overwhelming; and that inspectors should be given until the end of March or early April to carry out their task.[57]

152. Mr Blair suggested that, in the absence of a "smoking gun", Dr Blix would be able to harden up his findings on the basis of a pattern of non-co-operation from Iraq and that that would be sufficient for support for military action in the Security Council.

153. The US and UK should seek to persuade others, including Dr Blix, that that was the "true view" of resolution 1441.

154. Mr Blair used an interview on *Breakfast with Frost* on 26 January to set out the position that the inspections should be given sufficient time to determine whether or not Saddam Hussein was co-operating fully.[58] If he was not, that would be a sufficient reason for military action. A find of WMD was not required.

155. Mr Blair's proposed approach to his meeting with President Bush was discussed in a meeting of Ministers before Cabinet on 30 January and then discussed in general terms in Cabinet itself.

156. In a Note prepared before his meeting with President Bush on 31 January, Mr Blair proposed seeking a UN resolution on 5 March followed by an attempt to "mobilise Arab opinion to try to force Saddam out" before military action on 15 March.[59]

157. When Mr Blair met President Bush on 31 January, it was clear that the window of opportunity before the US took military action would be very short. The military campaign could begin "around 10 March".[60]

158. President Bush agreed to seek a second resolution to help Mr Blair, but there were major reservations within the US Administration about the wisdom of that approach.

159. Mr Blair confirmed that he was "solidly with the President and ready to do whatever it took to disarm Saddam" Hussein.

160. Reporting on his visit to Washington, Mr Blair told Parliament on 3 February 2003 that Saddam Hussein was not co-operating as required by resolution 1441 and, if that continued, a second resolution should be passed to confirm such a material breach.[61]

161. Mr Blair continued to set the need for action against Iraq in the context of the need to be seen to enforce the will of the UN and to deter future threats.

---

[57] Letter Manning to Rice, 24 January 2003, [untitled], attaching Note [Blair to Bush], [undated], 'Note'.
[58] *BBC News*, 26 January 2003, *Breakfast with Frost*.
[59] Note [Blair to Bush], [undated], 'Countdown'.
[60] Letter Manning to McDonald, 31 January 2003, 'Iraq: Prime Minister's Conversation with President Bush on 31 January'.
[61] House of Commons, *Official Report*, 3 February 2003, columns 21-38.

The gap between the Permanent Members of the Security Council widens

162. In their reports to the Security Council on 14 February:

- Dr Blix reported that UNMOVIC had not found any weapons of mass destruction and the items that were not accounted for might not exist, but Iraq needed to provide the evidence to answer the questions, not belittle them.

- Dr Mohamed ElBaradei, Director General of the International Atomic Energy Agency (IAEA), reported that the IAEA had found no evidence of ongoing prohibited nuclear or nuclear-related activities in Iraq although a number of issues were still under investigation.[62]

163. In the subsequent debate, members of the Security Council voiced widely divergent views.

164. Mr Annan concluded that there were real differences on strategy and timing in the Security Council. Iraq's non-co-operation was insufficient to bring members to agree that war was justified; they would only move if they came to their own judgement that inspections were pointless.[63]

165. On 19 February, Mr Blair sent President Bush a six-page Note. He proposed focusing on the absence of full co-operation and a "simple" resolution stating that Iraq had failed to take the final opportunity, with a side statement defining tough tests of co-operation and a vote on 14 March to provide a deadline for action.[64]

166. President Bush and Mr Blair agreed to introduce a draft resolution at the UN the following week but its terms were subject to further discussion.[65]

167. On 20 February, Mr Blair told Dr Blix that he wanted to offer the US an alternative strategy which included a deadline and tests for compliance.[66] He did not think Saddam Hussein would co-operate but he would try to get Dr Blix as much time as possible. Iraq could have signalled a change of heart in the December declaration. The Americans did not think that Saddam was going to co-operate: "Nor did he. But we needed to keep the international community together."

168. Dr Blix stated that full co-operation was a nebulous concept; and a deadline of 15 April would be too early. Dr Blix commented that "perhaps there was not much WMD in Iraq after all". Mr Blair responded that "even German and French intelligence were sure that there was WMD in Iraq". Dr Blix said they seemed "unsure" about "mobile BW

[62] UN Security Council, '4707th Meeting Friday 14 February 2003' (S/PV.4707).
[63] Telegram 268 UKMIS New York to FCO London, 15 February 2003, 'Foreign Secretary's Meeting with the UN Secretary-General: 14 February'.
[64] Letter Manning to Rice, 19 February 2003, 'Iraq' attaching Note [Blair to Bush], [undated], 'Note'.
[65] Letter Rycroft to McDonald, 19 February 2003, 'Iraq and MEPP: Prime Minister's Telephone Conversation with Bush, 19 February'.
[66] Letter Cannon to Owen, 20 February 2003, 'Iraq: Prime Minister's Conversation with Blix'.

production facilities": "It would be paradoxical and absurd if 250,000 men were to invade Iraq and find very little."

169. Mr Blair responded that "our intelligence was clear that Saddam had reconstituted his WMD programme".

170. On 24 February, the UK, US and Spain tabled a draft resolution stating that Iraq had failed to take the final opportunity offered by resolution 1441 and that the Security Council had decided to remain seized of the matter.[67] The draft failed to attract support.

171. France, Germany and Russia responded by tabling a memorandum, building on their tripartite declaration of 10 February, stating that "full and effective disarmament" remained "the imperative objective of the international community".[68] That "should be achieved peacefully through the inspection regime". The "conditions for using force" had "not been fulfilled". The Security Council "must step up its efforts to give a real chance to the peaceful settlement of the crisis".

172. On 25 February, Mr Blair told the House of Commons that the intelligence was "clear" that Saddam Hussein continued "to believe that his weapons of mass destruction programme is essential both for internal repression and for external aggression".[69] It was also "essential to his regional power". "Prior to the inspectors coming back in", Saddam Hussein "was engaged in a systematic exercise in concealment of those weapons". The inspectors had reported some co-operation on process, but had "denied progress on substance".

173. The House of Commons was asked on 26 February to reaffirm its endorsement of resolution 1441, support the Government's continuing efforts to disarm Iraq, and to call upon Iraq to recognise that this was its final opportunity to comply with its obligations.[70]

174. The Government motion was approved by 434 votes to 124; 199 MPs voted for an amendment which invited the House to "find the case for military action against Iraq as yet unproven".[71]

175. In a speech on 26 February, President Bush stated that the safety of the American people depended on ending the direct and growing threat from Iraq.[72]

176. President Bush also set out his hopes for the future of Iraq.

---

[67] Telegram 302 UKMIS New York to FCO London, 25 February 2003, 'Iraq: Tabling of US/UK/Spanish Draft Resolution: Draft Resolution'.
[68] UN Security Council, 24 February 2003, 'Letter dated 24 February 2003 from the Permanent Representatives of France, Germany and the Russian Federation to the United Nations addressed to the President of the Security Council' (S/2003/214).
[69] House of Commons, *Official Report*, 25 February 2003, columns 123-126.
[70] House of Commons, *Official Report*, 26 February 2003, column 265.
[71] House of Commons, *Official Report*, 26 February 2003, columns 367-371.
[72] The White House, 26 February 2003, *President discusses the future of Iraq*.

177. Reporting discussions in New York on 26 February, Sir Jeremy Greenstock wrote that there was "a general antipathy to having now to take decisions on this issue, and a wariness about what our underlying motives are behind the resolution".[73] Sir Jeremy concluded that the US was focused on preserving its room for manoeuvre while he was "concentrating on trying to win votes". It was the "middle ground" that mattered. Mexico and Chile were the "pivotal sceptics".

178. Lord Goldsmith told No.10 officials on 27 February that the safest legal course for future military action would be to secure a further Security Council resolution.[74] He had, however, reached the view that a "reasonable case" could be made that resolution 1441 was capable of reviving the authorisation to use force in resolution 678 (1990) without a further resolution, if there were strong factual grounds for concluding that Iraq had failed to take the final opportunity offered by resolution 1441.

179. Lord Goldsmith advised that, to avoid undermining the case for reliance on resolution 1441, it would be important to avoid giving any impression that the UK believed a second resolution was legally required.

180. Informal consultations in the Security Council on 27 February showed there was little support for the UK/US/Spanish draft resolution.[75]

181. An Arab League Summit on 1 March concluded that the crisis in Iraq must be resolved by peaceful means and in the framework of international legitimacy.[76]

182. Following his visit to Mexico, Sir David Manning concluded that Mexican support for a second resolution was "not impossible, but would not be easy and would almost certainly require some movement".[77]

183. During Sir David's visit to Chile, President Ricardo Lagos repeated his concerns, including the difficulty of securing nine votes or winning the presentational battle without further clarification of Iraq's non-compliance. He also suggested identifying benchmarks.[78]

184. Mr Blair wrote in his memoir that, during February, "despite his best endeavours", divisions in the Security Council had grown not reduced; and that the "dynamics of disagreement" were producing new alliances.[79] France, Germany and Russia were moving to create an alternative pole of power and influence.

---

[73] Telegram 314 UKMIS New York to FCO London, 27 February 2003, 'Iraq: 26 February'.
[74] Minute Brummell, 27 February 2003, 'Iraq: Attorney General's Meeting at No. 10 on 27th February 2003'.
[75] Telegram 318 UKMIS New York to FCO London, 28 February 2003, 'Iraq: 27 February Consultations and Missiles'.
[76] Telegram 68 Cairo to FCO London, 2 March 2003, 'Arab League Summit: Final Communique'.
[77] Telegram 1 Mexico City to Cabinet Office, 1 March 2003, 'Iraq: Mexico'.
[78] Telegram 34 Santiago to FCO London, 2 March 2003, 'Chile/Iraq: Visit by Manning and Scarlett'.
[79] Blair T. *A Journey*. Hutchinson, 2010.

185. Mr Blair thought that was "highly damaging" but "inevitable": "They felt as strongly as I did; and they weren't prepared to indulge the US, as they saw it."

186. Mr Blair concluded that for moral and strategic reasons the UK should be with the US and that:

> "... [W]e should make a last ditch attempt for a peaceful solution. First to make the moral case for removing Saddam ... Second, to try one more time to reunite the international community behind a clear base for action in the event of a continuing breach."

187. On 3 March, Mr Blair proposed an approach focused on setting a deadline of 17 March for Iraq to disclose evidence relating to the destruction of prohibited items and permit interviews; and an amnesty if Saddam Hussein left Iraq by 21 March.[80]

188. Mr Straw told Secretary Powell that the level of support in the UK for military action without a second resolution was palpably "very low". In that circumstance, even if a majority in the Security Council had voted for the resolution with only France exercising its veto, he was "increasingly pessimistic" about support within the Labour Party for military action.[81] The debate in the UK was:

> "... significantly defined by the tone of the debate in Washington and particularly remarks made by the President and others to the right of him, which suggested that the US would go to war whatever and was not bothered about a second resolution one way or another."

189. Following a discussion with Mr Blair, Mr Straw told Secretary Powell that Mr Blair:

> "... was concerned that, having shifted world (and British) public opinion over the months, it had now been seriously set back in recent days. We were not in the right position. The Prime Minister was considering a number of ideas which he might well put to the President."[82]

190. Mr Straw recorded that Secretary Powell had advised that, if Mr Blair wanted to make proposals, he should do so quickly. The US was not enthusiastic about the inclusion of an immunity clause for Saddam Hussein in the resolution.

191. Mr Straw reported that Secretary Powell had told President Bush that he judged a vetoed resolution would no longer be possible for the UK. Mr Straw said that without a second resolution approval for military action could be "beyond reach".

---

[80] Note (handwritten) [Blair], 3 March 2003, [untitled].
[81] Minute Straw to Prime Minister, 3 March 2003, 'Iraq: Second Resolution'.
[82] Letter Straw to Manning, 4 March 2003, 'Iraq: Conversation with Colin Powell, 3 March'.

192. Mr Straw told the Foreign Affairs Committee (FAC) on 4 March that it was "a matter of fact" that Iraq had been in material breach "for some weeks" and resolution 1441 provided sufficient legal authority to justify military action against Iraq if it was "in further material breach".[83]

193. Mr Straw also stated that a majority of members of the Security Council had been opposed to the suggestion that resolution 1441 should state explicitly that military action could be taken only if there were a second resolution.

194. Mr Blair was informed on the evening of 4 March that US military planners were looking at 12 March as the possible start date for the military campaign; and that Mr Geoff Hoon, the Defence Secretary, was concerned about the apparent disconnect with activity in the UN.[84]

195. Baroness Amos, Minister of State, Department for International Development (DFID), advised on 4 March that Angola, Cameroon and Guinea were not yet ready to commit to a "yes vote" and had emphasised the need for P5 unity.[85]

196. Sir Christopher Hum, British Ambassador to China, advised on 4 March that, if the resolution was put to a vote that day, China would abstain.[86]

197. Sir John Holmes, British Ambassador to France, advised on 4 March that France's main aim was to "avoid being put on the spot" by influencing the undecided, preventing the US and UK mustering nine votes, and keeping alongside the Russians and Chinese; and that there was "nothing that we can now do to dissuade them from this course".[87] Sir John also advised that "nothing the French say at this stage, even privately, should be taken at face value".

198. Mr Igor Ivanov, the Russian Foreign Minister, told Mr Straw on 4 March that Russia had failed in an attempt to persuade Saddam Hussein to leave and it would veto a resolution based on the draft circulated on 24 February.[88]

199. France, Germany and Russia stated on 5 March that they would not let a resolution pass that authorised the use of force.[89] Russia and France, "as Permanent Members of the Security Council, will assume all their responsibilities on this point".

---

[83] Minutes, Foreign Affairs Committee (House of Commons), 4 March 2003, [Evidence Session], Qs 151 and 154.
[84] Letter Watkins to Manning, 4 March 2003, 'Iraq: Timing of Military Action'.
[85] Minute Amos to Foreign Secretary, 4 March 2003, [untitled].
[86] Telegram 90 Beijing to FCO London, 4 March 2003, 'Iraq: Lobbying the Chinese'.
[87] Telegram 110 Paris to FCO London, 4 March 2003, 'Iraq: Avoiding a French Veto'.
[88] Telegram 37 FCO London to Moscow, 3 [sic] March 2003, 'Iraq: Foreign Secretary's Meetings with Russian Foreign Minister, 4 March'.
[89] *The Guardian*, 5 March 2003, *UN war doubters unite against resolution*; *The Guardian*, 6 March 2003, *Full text of Joint declaration*.

200. The British Embassy Washington reported overnight on 5/6 March that "barring a highly improbable volte face by Saddam", the US was now firmly on track for military action and would deal firmly with any efforts in the UN to slow down the timetable.[90]

201. The Embassy reported that the only event which might significantly affect the US timetable would be problems for the UK. That had been described as "huge – like trying to play football without the quarterback". The US was "therefore pulling out all the stops at the UN". The US fully understood the importance of the second resolution for the UK.

202. Sir Jeremy Greenstock advised that the US would not countenance the use of benchmarks. That risked delaying the military timetable.[91]

203. Mr Blair told Cabinet on 6 March that the argument boiled down to the question of whether Saddam Hussein would ever voluntarily co-operate with the UN to disarm Iraq.[92]

204. Mr Blair concluded that it was for the Security Council to determine whether Iraq was co-operating fully.

205. In his discussions with President Lagos on 6 March, Mr Blair stated that the US would go ahead without the UN if asked to delay military action until April or May.[93]

206. In his report to the Security Council on 7 March, Dr Blix stated that there had been an acceleration of initiatives from Iraq since the end of January, but they could not be said to constitute immediate co-operation.[94] Nor did they necessarily cover all areas of relevance; but they were nevertheless welcome. UNMOVIC was drawing up a work programme of key disarmament tasks, which would be ready later that month, for approval by the Security Council. It would take "months" to complete the programme.

207. Dr ElBaradei reported that there were no indications that Iraq had resumed nuclear activities since the inspectors left in December 1998 and the recently increased level of Iraqi co-operation should allow the IAEA to provide the Security Council with an assessment of Iraq's nuclear capabilities in the near future.

208. There was unanimity in calls for Iraq to increase its co-operation. But there was a clear division between the US, UK, Spain and Bulgaria who spoke in favour of a further resolution and France, Germany, Russia and China and most other Member States who spoke in favour of continuing to pursuing disarmament through strengthened inspections.

209. The UK, US and Spain circulated a revised draft resolution deciding that Iraq would have failed to take the final opportunity offered by resolution 1441 (2002) unless

---

[90] Telegram 294 Washington to FCO London, 6 March 2003, 'Personal Iraq: UN Endgame'.
[91] Telegram 353 UKMIS New York to FCO London, 6 March 2003, 'Iraq: 5 March'.
[92] Cabinet Conclusions, 6 March 2003.
[93] Letter Cannon to Owen, 6 March 2003, 'Iraq: Prime Minister's Conversation with President of Chile, 6 March'.
[94] UN Security Council, '4714th Meeting Friday 7 March 2003' (S/PV.4714).

the Council concluded, on or before 17 March 2003, that Iraq had demonstrated full, unconditional, immediate and active co-operation in accordance with its disarmament obligations and was yielding possession of all weapons and proscribed material to UNMOVIC and the IAEA.

210. President Putin told Mr Blair on 7 March that Russia would oppose military action.[95]

211. Mr Straw told Mr Annan that military considerations could not be allowed "to dictate policy", but the military build-up "could not be maintained for ever", and:

> "... the more he had looked into the Iraq dossier [issue] the more convinced he had become of the need for action. Reading the clusters document [a report of outstanding issues produced by UNMOVIC on 7 March] made his hair stand on end."[96]

212. Mr Straw set out the UK thinking on a deadline, stating that this was "Iraq's last chance", but the objective was disarmament and, if Saddam Hussein did what was demanded, "he could stay". In those circumstances, a "permanent and toughened inspections regime" would be needed, possibly "picking up some earlier ideas for an all-Iraq NFZ".

213. Lord Goldsmith sent his formal advice to Mr Blair on 7 March.[97]

The end of the UN route

214. When Mr Blair spoke to President Bush at 6pm on 7 March he emphasised the importance of securing nine positive votes[98] in the Security Council for Parliamentary approval for UK military action.[99]

215. Mr Blair argued that while the 17 March deadline in the draft resolution was not sufficient for Iraq to disarm fully, it was sufficient to make a judgement on whether Saddam Hussein had had a change of heart. If Iraq started to co-operate, the inspectors could have as much time as they liked.

216. In a last attempt to move opinion and secure the support of nine members of the Security Council, Mr Blair decided on 8 March to propose a short extension of the timetable beyond 17 March and to revive the idea of producing a "side statement" setting out a series of tests which would provide the basis for a judgement on Saddam Hussein's intentions.

---

[95] Letter Rycroft to McDonald, 7 March 2003, 'Iraq: Prime Minister's Conversation with President Putin, 7 March'.
[96] Telegram 366 UKMIS New York to FCO London, 7 March 2003, 'Iraq: Foreign Secretary's Meeting with UN Secretary-General, New York, 6 March'.
[97] Minute Goldsmith to Prime Minister, 7 March 2003, 'Iraq: Resolution 1441'.
[98] The number of votes required, in the absence of a veto from one or more of the five Permanent Members, for a decision to take action with the authority of the Security Council.
[99] Letter Rycroft to McDonald, 7 March 2003, 'Iraq: Prime Minister's Conversation with Bush, 7 March'.

217. The initiative was pursued through intensive diplomatic activity to lobby for support between London and the capitals of Security Council Member States.

218. Mr Blair told the Inquiry:

"It was worth having one last-ditch chance to see if you could bring people back together on the same page ... [W]hat President Bush had to do was agree to table a fresh resolution. What the French had to agree was you couldn't have another resolution and another breach and no action. So my idea was define the circumstances of breach – that was the tests that we applied with Hans Blix – get the Americans to agree to the resolution, get the French to agree that you couldn't just go back to the same words of 1441 again, you had to take it a stage further."[100]

219. In a discussion on 9 March, Mr Blair told President Bush that he needed a second resolution to secure Parliamentary support for UK involvement in military action.[101] He sought President Bush's support for setting out tests in a side statement, including that the vote in the Security Council might have to be delayed "by a couple of days".

220. President Bush was unwilling to countenance delay. He was reported to have told Mr Blair that, if the second resolution failed, he would find another way to involve the UK.

221. Mr Blair told President Bush the UK would be with the US in taking action if he (Mr Blair) possibly could be.

222. Sir Jeremy Greenstock reported that Dr Blix was prepared to work with the UK on identifying tests but had reminded him that UNMOVIC still lacked clear evidence that Iraq possessed any WMD.[102]

223. Mr Blair spoke twice to President Lagos on 10 March in an attempt to find a path that President Lagos and President Vicente Fox of Mexico could support.

224. In the second conversation, Mr Blair said that he thought it "would be possible to find different wording" on the ultimatum to Iraq. Timing "would be difficult, but he would try to get some flexibility" if the first two issues "fell into place".[103]

225. Mr Straw reported that Secretary Powell thought that there were seven solid votes, and uncertainty about Mexico, Chile and Pakistan.[104] If there were fewer than nine, the second resolution should not be put to the vote.

---

[100] Public hearing, 29 January 2010, page 127.
[101] Letter Rycroft to McDonald, 9 March 2003, 'Iraq: Prime Minister's Conversation with Bush, 9 March'.
[102] Telegram 391 UKMIS New York to FCO London, 10 March 2003, 'Iraq: Second Resolution'.
[103] Letter Rycroft to McDonald, 10 March 2003, 'Iraq: Prime Minister's Phone Calls with Lagos, Bush and Aznar, 10 March'.
[104] Letter Straw to Manning, 11 March 2003, 'Conversation with US Secretary of State, 10 March'.

226. Mr Straw replied that "he was increasingly coming to the view that we should not push the matter to a vote if we were going to be vetoed"; but that had not yet been agreed by Mr Blair.

227. By 10 March, President Bush's position was hardening and he was very reluctant to delay military action.

228. When Mr Blair spoke to President Bush, they discussed the "seven solid votes" for the resolution.[105]

229. Mr Alastair Campbell, Mr Blair's Director of Communications and Strategy, wrote that Mr Blair had done most of the talking.[106] President Bush thought President Jacques Chirac of France was "trying to get us to the stage where we would not put [the resolution] to a vote because we would be so worried about losing".

230. Mr Blair had argued that if Chile and Mexico could be shifted, that would "change the weather". If France and Russia then vetoed the resolution but the "numbers were right on the UN", Mr Blair thought that he would "have a fighting chance of getting it through the Commons". Subsequently, Mr Blair suggested that a change in Chile and Mexico's position might be used to influence President Putin.

231. President Bush was "worried about rolling in more time" but Mr Blair had "held his ground", arguing that Chile and Mexico would "need to be able to point to something that they won last minute that explains why they finally supported us". President Bush "said 'Let me be frank. The second resolution is for the benefit of Great Britain. We would want it so we can go ahead together.'" President Bush's position was that the US and UK "must not retreat from 1441 and we cannot keep giving them more time"; it was "time to do this" and there should be "no more deals".

232. Sir David Manning sent the UK proposals for a revised deadline, and a side statement identifying six tests on which Saddam Hussein's intentions would be judged, to Dr Condoleezza Rice, President Bush's National Security Advisor, and to President Lagos.[107]

233. Mr Blair wrote in his memoir that President Bush and his military were concerned about delay.[108]

> "It [the proposal for tests/more time] was indeed a hard sell to George. His system was completely against it. His military were, not unreasonably, fearing that delay gave the enemy time – and time could mean a tougher struggle and more lives lost.

---

[105] Letter Rycroft to McDonald, 10 March 2003, 'Iraq: Prime Minister's Phone Calls with Lagos, Bush and Aznar, 10 March'.
[106] Campbell A & Hagerty B. *The Alastair Campbell Diaries. Volume 4. The Burden of Power: Countdown to Iraq.* Hutchinson, 2012.
[107] Letter Manning to Rice, 10 March 2003, [untitled].
[108] Blair T. *A Journey*. Hutchinson, 2010.

This was also troubling my military. We had all sorts of contingency plans in place ... There was both UK and US intelligence warning us of the risk.

"Nonetheless I thought it was worth a try ..."

234. Mr Blair also wrote:

"Chile and Mexico were prepared to go along, but only up to a point. Ricardo made it clear that if there was heavy opposition from France, it would be tough for them to participate in what would then be a token vote, incapable of being passed because of a veto – and what's more, a veto not by Russia, but by France.

"Unfortunately, the French position had, if anything, got harder not softer. They were starting to say they would not support military action in any circumstances, irrespective of what the inspectors found ..."

235. In a press conference on 10 March, Mr Annan reiterated the Security Council's determination to disarm Iraq, but said that every avenue for a peaceful resolution of the crisis had to be exhausted before force should be used.[109]

236. Mr Annan also warned that, if the Security Council failed to agree on a common position and action was taken without the authority of the Council, the legitimacy and support for any such action would be seriously impaired.

237. In an interview on 10 March, President Chirac stated that it was for the inspectors to advise whether they could complete their task.[110] If they reported that they were not in a position to guarantee Iraq's disarmament, it would be:

"... for the Security Council alone to decide the right thing to do. But in that case ... regrettably, the war would become inevitable. It isn't today."

238. President Chirac stated that he did not consider that the draft resolution tabled by the US, UK and Spain would attract support from nine members of the Security Council. In that case, there would be no majority for action, "So there won't be a veto problem."

239. But if there were a majority "in favour of the new resolution", France would "vote 'no'".

240. In response to a question asking, "And, this evening, this is your position in principle?", President Chirac responded:

"My position is that, regardless of the circumstances, France will vote 'no' because she considers this evening that there are no grounds for waging war in order to achieve the goal we have set ourselves, that is to disarm Iraq."

---

[109] United Nations, 10 March 2003, *Secretary-General's press conference (unofficial transcript)*.
[110] The Élysée, *Interview télévisée de Jacques Chirac, le 10 mars 2003*. A translation for HMG was produced in a Note, [unattributed and undated], 'Iraq – Interview given by M. Jacques Chirac, President of the Republic, to French TV (10 March 2003)'.

241. By 11 March, it was clear that, in the time available before the US was going to take military action, it would be difficult to secure nine votes in the Security Council for a resolution determining that Iraq had failed to take the final opportunity offered by resolution 1441.

242. Mr Straw wrote to Mr Blair on 11 March setting out his firm conclusion that:

"If we cannot gain nine votes <u>and</u> be sure of no veto, we should not push our second resolution to a vote. The political and diplomatic consequences for the UK would be significantly worse to have our ... resolution defeated ... than if we camp on 1441 ..."[111]

243. Mr Straw set out his reasoning in some detail, including that:

- Although in earlier discussion he had "warmed to the idea" that it was worth pushing the issue to a vote "if we had nine votes and faced only a French veto", the more he "thought about this, the worse an idea it becomes".

- A veto by France only was "in practice less likely than two or even three vetoes".

- The "best, least risky way to gain a moral majority" was "by the 'Kosovo route' – essentially what I am recommending. The key to our moral legitimacy then was the matter never went to a vote – but everyone knew the reason for this was that Russia would have vetoed."

244. Mr Straw suggested that the UK should adopt a strategy based on the argument that Iraq had failed to take the final opportunity offered by resolution 1441, and that the last three meetings of the Security Council met the requirement for Security Council consideration of reports of non-compliance.

245. Mr Straw also identified the need for a "Plan B" for the UK not to participate in military action in the event that the Government failed to secure a majority in the Parliamentary Labour Party for military action.

246. Mr Straw concluded:

"We will obviously need to discuss all this, but I thought it best to put it in your mind as event[s] could move fast. And what I propose is a great deal better than the alternatives. When Bush graciously accepted your offer to be with him all the way, he wanted you alive not dead!"

247. There was no reference in the minute to President Chirac's remarks the previous evening.

---

[111] Minute Straw to Prime Minister, 11 March 2003, 'Iraq: What if We Cannot Win the Second Resolution?'

248. When Mr Blair and President Bush discussed the position late on 11 March, it was clear that President Bush was determined not to postpone the start of military action.[112] They discussed the impact of President Chirac's "veto threats". Mr Blair considered that President Chirac's remarks "gave some cover" for ending the UN route.

249. Reporting discussions in New York on 11 March on the draft resolution and details of a possible "side statement", Sir Jeremy Greenstock advised that the draft resolution tabled by the UK, US and Spain on 7 March had "no chance ... of adoption".[113]

250. In a telephone call with President Bush on 12 March, Mr Blair proposed that the US and UK should continue to seek a compromise in the UN, while confirming that he knew it would not happen. He would say publicly that the French had prevented them from securing a resolution, so there would not be one.[114]

251. Mr Blair wanted to avoid a gap between the end of the negotiating process and the Parliamentary vote in which France or another member of the Security Council might table a resolution that attracted the support of a majority of the Council. That could have undermined the UK (and US) position on its legal basis for action.

252. When he discussed the options with Mr Straw early on 12 March, Mr Blair decided that the UK would continue to support the US.[115]

253. During Prime Minister's Questions on 12 March, Mr Blair stated:

"I hope that even now those countries that are saying they would use their veto no matter what the circumstances will reconsider and realise that by doing so they put at risk not just the disarmament of Saddam, but the unity of the United Nations."[116]

254. The FCO assessed on 12 March that the votes of the three African states were reasonably secure but Pakistan's vote was not so certain. It was hoped that the six tests plus a short extension of the 17 March deadline might deliver Mexico and Chile.[117]

255. The UK circulated its draft side statement setting out the six tests to a meeting of Security Council members in New York on the evening of 12 March.[118]

256. Sir Jeremy Greenstock told Council members that the UK "non-paper" responded to an approach from the "undecided six"[119] looking for a way forward, setting out six

---

[112] Letter Cannon to McDonald, 11 March 2003, 'Iraq: Prime Minister's Conversations with Bush and Lagos, 11 March'.
[113] Telegram 417 UKMIS New York to FCO London, 12 March 2003, 'Personal Iraq: Side Statement and End Game Options'.
[114] Letter Rycroft to McDonald, 12 March 2003, 'Iraq: Prime Minister's Telephone Conversation with President Bush, 12 March'.
[115] Public hearing, 21 January 2010, page 105.
[116] House of Commons, *Official Report*, 12 March 2003, column 288.
[117] Telegram 33 FCO London to Riyadh, 12 March 2003, 'Personal for Heads of Mission: Iraq: The Endgame'.
[118] Telegram 429 UKMIS New York to FCO London, 13 March 2003, 'Iraq: UK Side-Statement'.
[119] Angola, Cameroon, Chile, Guinea, Mexico, Pakistan.

tasks to be achieved in a 10-day timeline.[120] Sir Jeremy reported that France, Germany and Russia all said that the draft resolution without operative paragraph 3 would still authorise force. The UK had not achieved "any kind of breakthrough" and there were "serious questions about the available time", which the US would "not help us to satisfy".

257. Mr Blair told Cabinet on 13 March that work continued in the UN to obtain a second resolution and, following the French decision to veto, the outcome remained open.[121]

258. Mr Straw described President Chirac's position as "irresponsible".

259. Mr Straw told Cabinet that there was "good progress" in gaining support in the Security Council.

260. Mr Blair concluded that the French position "looked to be based on a calculation of strategic benefit". It was "in contradiction of the Security Council's earlier view that military action would follow if Iraq did not fully and unconditionally co-operate with the inspectors". The UK would "continue to show flexibility" in its efforts to achieve a second resolution and, "if France could be shown to be intransigent, the mood of the Security Council could change towards support for the British draft".

261. Mr Blair agreed the military plan later on 13 March.[122]

262. On 13 March, Mr Blair and President Bush discussed withdrawing the resolution on 17 March followed by a US ultimatum to Saddam Hussein to leave within 48 hours. There would be no US military action until after the vote in the House of Commons on 18 March.[123]

263. Mr Blair continued to press President Bush to publish the Road Map on the Middle East Peace Process because of its impact on domestic opinion in the UK as well as its strategic impact.

264. Reporting developments in New York on 13 March, Sir Jeremy Greenstock warned that the UK tests had attracted no support, and that the US might be ready to call a halt to the UN process on 15 March.[124] The main objections had included the "perceived authorisation of force in the draft resolution" and a desire to wait for UNMOVIC's own list of key tasks which would be issued early the following week.

265. President Chirac told Mr Blair on 14 March that France was "content to proceed 'in the logic of UNSCR 1441'; but it could not accept an ultimatum or any 'automaticity' of recourse to force".[125] He proposed looking at a new resolution in line with

---

[120] Telegram 428 UKMIS New York to FCO London, 13 March 2003, 'Iraq: UK Circulates Side-Statement'.
[121] Cabinet Conclusions, 13 March 2003.
[122] Letter Rycroft to Watkins, 13 March 2003, 'Iraq: Military Planning'.
[123] Letter Cannon to McDonald, 13 March 2003, 'Iraq: Military Timetable'.
[124] Telegram 438 UKMIS New York to FCO London, 14 March 2003, 'Iraq: 13 March'.
[125] Letter Cannon to Owen, 14 March 2003, 'Iraq: Prime Minister's Conversation with President Chirac, 14 March'.

resolution 1441, "provided that it excluded these options". President Chirac "suggested that the UNMOVIC work programme might provide a way forward. France was prepared to look at reducing the 120 day timeframe it envisaged."

266. In response to a question from President Chirac about whether it would be the inspectors or the Security Council who decided whether Saddam had co-operated, Mr Blair "insisted that it must be the Security Council".

267. President Chirac agreed, "although the Security Council should make its judgement on the basis of the inspectors' report". He "wondered whether it would be worth" Mr Straw and Mr Dominique de Villepin, the French Foreign Minister, "discussing the situation to see if we could find some flexibility"; or was it "too late"?

268. Mr Blair said, "every avenue must be explored".

269. In the subsequent conversation with President Bush about the French position and what to say when the resolution was pulled, Mr Blair proposed that they would need to show that France would not authorise the use of force in any circumstances.[126]

270. President Lagos initially informed Mr Blair on 14 March that the UK proposals did not have Chile's support and that he was working on other ideas.[127] He subsequently informed Mr Blair that he would not pursue his proposals unless Mr Blair or President Bush asked him to.

271. Mr Tony Brenton, Chargé d'Affaires, British Embassy Washington, reported that President Bush was determined to remove Saddam Hussein and to stick to the US timetable for action. The UK's "steadfastness" had been "invaluable" in bringing in other countries in support of action.[128]

272. In a declaration on 15 March, France, with Germany and Russia, attempted to secure support in the Security Council for continued inspections.[129]

273. At the Azores Summit on 16 March, President Bush, Mr Blair and Prime Minister José María Aznar of Spain agreed that, unless there was a fundamental change in the next 24 hours, the UN process would end.[130]

274. In public, the focus was on a "last chance for peace". The joint communiqué contained a final appeal to Saddam Hussein to comply with his obligations and to the Security Council to back a second resolution containing an ultimatum.

---

[126] Letter Rycroft to McDonald, 14 March 2003, 'Iraq: Prime Minister's Conversation with Bush, 14 March'.
[127] Letter [Francis] Campbell to Owen, 14 March 2003, 'Iraq: Prime Minister's Conversation with President Lagos of Chile, 14 March'.
[128] Telegram 350 Washington to FCO London, 15 March 2003, 'Iraq'.
[129] UN Security Council, 18 March 2003, 'Letter dated 15 March 2003 from the Permanent Representative of Germany to the United Nations addressed to the President of the Security Council' (S/2003/320).
[130] Letter Manning to McDonald, 16 March 2013, 'Iraq: Summit Meeting in the Azores: 16 March'.

275. In his memoir, Mr Blair wrote:

> "So when I look back ... I know there was never any way Britain was not going to be with the US at that moment, once we went down the UN route and Saddam was in breach. Of course such a statement is always subject to *in extremis* correction. A crazy act of aggression? No, we would not have supported that. But given the history, you couldn't call Saddam a crazy target.

> "Personally I have little doubt that at some point we would have to have dealt with him ..."[131]

276. At "about 3.15pm UK time" on 17 March, Sir Jeremy Greenstock announced that the resolution would not be put to a vote, stating that the co-sponsors reserved the right to take their own steps to secure the disarmament of Iraq.[132]

277. The subsequent discussion in the Council suggested that only the UK, the US, and Spain took the view that all options other than the use of military force had been exhausted.[133]

278. A specially convened Cabinet at 1600 on 17 March 2003 endorsed the decision that the diplomatic process was now at an end and Saddam Hussein should be given an ultimatum to leave Iraq; and that the House of Commons would be asked to endorse the use of military action against Iraq to enforce compliance, if necessary.[134]

279. In his statement to the House of Commons that evening, Mr Straw said that the Government had reluctantly concluded that France's actions had put a consensus in the Security Council on a further resolution "beyond reach".[135]

280. As a result of Saddam Hussein's persistent refusal to meet the UN's demands, the Cabinet had decided to ask the House of Commons to support the UK's participation in military action, should that be necessary to achieve the disarmament of Iraq "and thereby the maintenance of the authority of the United Nations".

281. Mr Straw stated that Lord Goldsmith's Written Answer "set out the legal basis for the use of force".

282. Mr Straw drew attention to the significance of the fact that no one "in discussions in the Security Council and outside" had claimed that Iraq was in full compliance with its obligations.

283. In a statement later that evening, Mr Robin Cook, the Leader of the House of Commons, set out his doubts about the degree to which Saddam Hussein posed a

---

[131] Blair T. *A Journey*. Hutchinson, 2010.
[132] Telegram 465 UKMIS New York to FCO London, 18 March 2003, 'Iraq: Resolution: Statement'.
[133] Telegram 464 UKMIS New York to FCO London, 18 March 2003, 'Iraq: Resolution'.
[134] Cabinet Conclusions, 17 March 2003.
[135] House of Commons, *Official Report*, 17 March 2003, columns 703-705.

"clear and present danger" and his concerns that the UK was being "pushed too quickly into conflict" by the US without the support of the UN and in the face of hostility from many of the UK's traditional allies.[136]

284. On 17 March, President Bush issued an ultimatum giving Saddam Hussein 48 hours to leave Iraq.

285. The French President's office issued a statement early on 18 March stating that the US ultimatum was a unilateral decision going against the will of the international community who wanted to pursue Iraqi disarmament in accordance with resolution 1441.[137] It stated:

> "... only the Security Council is authorised to legitimise the use of force. France appeals to the responsibility of all to see that international legality is respected. To disregard the legitimacy of the UN, to favour force over the law, would be to take on a heavy responsibility."

286. On the evening of 18 March, the House of Commons passed by 412 votes to 149 a motion supporting "the decision of Her Majesty's Government that the United Kingdom should use all means necessary to ensure the disarmament of Iraq's weapons of mass destruction".

287. President Bush wrote in his memoir that he convened "the entire National Security Council" on the morning of 19 March where he "gave the order to launch Operation Iraqi Freedom".[138]

288. In the Security Council debate on 19 March, the majority of members of the Security Council, including France, Russia and China, made clear that they thought the goal of disarming Iraq could be achieved by peaceful means and emphasised the primary responsibility of the Security Council for the maintenance of international peace and security.[139]

289. UNMOVIC and the IAEA had provided the work programmes required by resolution 1284. They included 12 key tasks identified by UNMOVIC where progress "could have an impact on the Council's assessment of co-operation of Iraq".

290. Shortly before midnight on 19 March, the US informed Sir David Manning that there was to be a change to the plan and US airstrikes would be launched at 0300 GMT on 20 March.[140]

---

[136] House of Commons, *Official Report*, 17 March 2003, columns 726-728.
[137] Telegram 135 Paris to FCO London, 18 March 2003, 'Iraq: Chirac's Reaction to Ultimatum'.
[138] Bush GW. *Decision Points*. Virgin Books, 2010.
[139] UN Security Council, '4721st Meeting Wednesday 19 March 2003' (S/PV.4721).
[140] Letter Manning to McDonald, 20 March 2003, 'Iraq'.

291. Early on the morning of 20 March, US forces crossed into Iraq and seized the port area of Umm Qasr.[141]

292. Mr Blair continued to state that France was responsible for the impasse.

293. At Cabinet on 20 March, Mr Blair concluded that the Government:

> "... should lose no opportunity to propagate the reason, at every level and as widely as possible, why we had arrived at a diplomatic impasse, and why it was necessary to take action against Iraq. France had not been prepared to accept that Iraq's failure to comply with its obligations should lead to the use of force to achieve compliance."[142]

Why Iraq? Why now?

294. In his memoir, Mr Blair described his speech opening the debate on 18 March as "the most important speech I had ever made".[143]

295. Mr Blair framed the decision for the House of Commons as a "tough" and "stark" choice between "retreat" and holding firm to the course of action the Government had set. Mr Blair stated that he believed "passionately" in the latter. He deployed a wide range of arguments to explain the grounds for military action and to make a persuasive case for the Government's policy.[144]

296. In setting out his position, Mr Blair recognised the gravity of the debate and the strength of opposition in both the country and Parliament to immediate military action. In his view, the issue mattered "so much" because the outcome would not just determine the fate of the Iraqi regime and the Iraqi people but would:

> "... determine the way in which Britain and the world confront the central security threat of the 21st century, the development of the United Nations, the relationship between Europe and the United States, the relations within the European Union and the way in which the United States engages with the rest of the world. So it could hardly be more important. It will determine the pattern of international politics for the next generation."

Was Iraq a serious or imminent threat?

297. On 18 March 2003, the House of Commons was asked:

- to recognise that Iraq's weapons of mass destruction and long-range missiles, and its continuing non-compliance with Security Council resolutions, posed a threat to international peace and security; and

---

[141] Ministry of Defence, *Operations in Iraq: Lessons for the Future*, December 2003, page 12.
[142] Cabinet Conclusions, 20 March 2003.
[143] Blair T. *A Journey*. Hutchinson, 2010.
[144] House of Commons, *Official Report*, 18 March 2003, columns 760-774.

- to support the use of all means necessary to ensure the disarmament of Iraq's weapons of mass destruction, on the basis that the United Kingdom must uphold the authority of the United Nations as set out in resolution 1441 and many resolutions preceding it.

298. In his statement, Mr Blair addressed both the threat to international peace and security presented by Iraq's defiance of the UN and its failure to comply with its disarmament obligations as set out in resolution 1441 (2002). Iraq was "the test of whether we treat the threat seriously".

299. Mr Blair rehearsed the Government's position on Iraq's past pursuit and use of weapons of mass destruction; its failures to comply with the obligations imposed by the UN Security Council between 1991 and 1998; Iraq's repeated declarations which proved to be false; and the "large quantities of weapons of mass destruction" which were "unaccounted for". He described UNSCOM's final report (in January 1999) as "a withering indictment of Saddam's lies, deception and obstruction".

300. Mr Blair cited the UNMOVIC "clusters" document issued on 7 March as "a remarkable document", detailing "all the unanswered questions about Iraq's weapons of mass destruction", listing "29 different areas in which the inspectors have been unable to obtain information".

301. He stated that, based on Iraq's false declaration, its failure to co-operate, the unanswered questions in the UNMOVIC "clusters" document, and the unaccounted for material, the Security Council should have convened and condemned Iraq as in material breach of its obligations. If Saddam Hussein continued to fail to co-operate, force should be used.

302. Addressing the wider message from the issue of Iraq, Mr Blair asked:

"... what ... would any tyrannical regime possessing weapons of mass destruction think when viewing the history of the world's diplomatic dance with Saddam over ... 12 years? That our capacity to pass firm resolutions has only been matched by our feebleness in implementing them."

303. Mr Blair acknowledged that Iraq was "not the only country with weapons of mass destruction", but declared: "back away from this confrontation now, and future conflicts will be infinitely worse and more devastating in their effects".

304. Mr Blair added:

"The real problem is that ... people dispute Iraq is a threat, dispute the link between terrorism and weapons of mass destruction, and dispute in other words, the whole basis of our assertion that the two together constitute a fundamental assault on our way of life."

305. Mr Blair also described a "threat of chaos and disorder" arising from "tyrannical regimes with weapons of mass destruction and extreme terrorist groups" prepared to use them.

306. Mr Blair set out his concerns about:

- proliferators of nuclear equipment or expertise;
- "dictatorships with highly repressive regimes" who were "desperately trying to acquire" chemical, biological or, "particularly, nuclear weapons capability" – some of those were "a short time away from having a serviceable nuclear weapon", and that activity was increasing, not diminishing; and
- the possibility of terrorist groups obtaining and using weapons of mass destruction, including a "radiological bomb".

307. Those two threats had very different motives and different origins. He accepted "fully" that the association between the two was:

"... loose – but it is hardening. The possibility of the two coming together – of terrorist groups in possession of weapons of mass destruction or even of a so called dirty radiological bomb – is now in my judgement, a real and present danger to Britain and its national security."

308. Later in his speech, Mr Blair stated that the threat which Saddam Hussein's arsenal posed:

"... to British citizens at home and abroad cannot simply be contained. Whether in the hands of his regime or in the hands of the terrorists to whom he would give his weapons, they pose a clear danger to British citizens ..."

309. This fusion of long-standing concerns about proliferation with the post-9/11 concerns about mass-casualty terrorism was at the heart of the Government's case for taking action at this time against Iraq.

310. The UK assessment of Iraq's capabilities set out in Section 4 of the Report shows:

- The proliferation of nuclear, chemical and biological weapons and their delivery systems, particularly ballistic missiles, was regarded as a major threat. But Iran, North Korea and Libya were of greater concern than Iraq in terms of the risk of nuclear and missile proliferation.
- JIC Assessments, reflected in the September 2002 dossier, had consistently taken the view that, if sanctions were removed or became ineffective, it would take Iraq at least five years following the end of sanctions to produce enough fissile material for a weapon. On 7 March, the IAEA had reported to the Security Council that there was no indication that Iraq had resumed its nuclear activities.
- The September dossier stated that Iraq could produce a nuclear weapon within one to two years if it obtained fissile material and other essential components

from a foreign supplier. There was no evidence that Iraq had tried to acquire fissile material and other components or – were it able to do so – that it had the technical capabilities to turn these materials into a usable weapon.

- JIC Assessments had identified the possible stocks of chemical and biological weapons which would largely have been for short-range, battlefield use by the Iraqi armed forces. The JIC had also judged in the September dossier that Iraq was producing chemical and biological agents and that there were development programmes for longer-range missiles capable of delivering them.

- Iraq's proscribed Al Samoud 2 missiles were being destroyed.

311. The UK Government did have significant concerns about the potential risks of all types of weapons of mass destruction being obtained by Islamist extremists (in particular Al Qaida) who would be prepared to use such weapons.

312. Saddam Hussein's regime had the potential to proliferate material and know-how, to terrorist groups, but it was not judged likely to do so.

313. On 28 November 2001, the JIC assessed that:

- Saddam Hussein had "refused to permit any Al Qaida presence in Iraq".

- Evidence of contact between Iraq and Usama Bin Laden (UBL) was "fragmentary and uncorroborated"; including that Iraq had been in contact with Al Qaida for exploratory discussions on toxic materials in late 1988.

- "With common enemies ... there was clearly scope for collaboration."

- There was "no evidence that these contacts led to practical co-operation; we judge it unlikely ... There is no evidence UBL's organisation has ever had a presence in Iraq."

- Practical co-operation between Iraq and Al Qaida was "unlikely because of mutual mistrust".

- There was "no credible evidence of covert transfers of WMD-related technology and expertise to terrorist groups".[145]

314. On 29 January 2003, the JIC assessed that, despite the presence of terrorists in Iraq "with links to Al Qaida", there was "no intelligence of current co-operation between Iraq and Al Qaida".[146]

315. On 10 February 2003, the JIC judged that Al Qaida would "not carry out attacks under Iraqi direction".[147]

[145] JIC Assessment, 28 November 2001, 'Iraq after September 11 – The Terrorist Threat'.
[146] JIC Assessment, 29 January 2003, 'Iraq: The Emerging view from Baghdad'.
[147] JIC Assessment, 10 February 2003, 'International Terrorism: War with Iraq'

316. Sir Richard Dearlove told the Inquiry:

"... I don't think the Prime Minister ever accepted the link between Iraq and terrorism. I think it would be fair to say that the Prime Minister was very worried about the possible conjunction of terrorism and WMD, but not specifically in relation to Iraq ... [I] think, one could say this is one of his primary national security concerns given the nature of Al Qaida."[148]

317. The JIC assessed that Iraq was likely to mount a terrorist attack only in response to military action and if the existence of the regime was threatened.

318. The JIC Assessment of 10 October 2002 stated that Saddam Hussein's "overriding objective" was to "avoid a US attack that would threaten his regime".[149] The JIC judged that, in the event of US-led military action against Iraq, Saddam would:

"... aim to use terrorism or the threat of it. Fearing the US response, he is likely to weigh the costs and benefits carefully in deciding the timing and circumstances in which terrorism is used. But intelligence on Iraq's capabilities and intentions in this field is limited."

319. The JIC also judged that:

- Saddam's "capability to conduct effective terrorist attacks" was "very limited".
- Iraq's "terrorism capability" was "inadequate to carry out chemical or biological attacks beyond individual assassination attempts using poisons".

320. The JIC Assessment of 29 January 2003 sustained its earlier judgements on Iraq's ability and intent to conduct terrorist operations.[150]

321. Sir David Omand, the Security and Intelligence Co-ordinator in the Cabinet Office from 2002 to 2005, told the Inquiry that, in March 2002, the Security Service judged that the "threat from terrorism from Saddam's own intelligence apparatus in the event of an intervention in Iraq ... was judged to be limited and containable".[151]

322. Baroness Manningham-Buller, the Director General of the Security Service from 2002 to 2007, confirmed that position, stating that the Security Service felt there was "a pretty good intelligence picture of a threat from Iraq within the UK and to British interests".[152]

---

[148] Private hearing, 16 June 2010, pages 39-40.
[149] JIC Assessment, 10 October 2002, 'International Terrorism: The Threat from Iraq'.
[150] JIC Assessment, 29 January 2003, 'Iraq: The Emerging view from Baghdad'.
[151] Public hearing, 20 January 2010, page 37.
[152] Public hearing, 20 July 2010, page 6.

323. Baroness Manningham-Buller added that subsequent events showed the judgement that Saddam Hussein did not have the capability to do anything much in the UK, had "turned out to be the right judgement".[153]

324. While it was reasonable for the Government to be concerned about the fusion of proliferation and terrorism, there was no basis in the JIC Assessments to suggest that Iraq itself represented such a threat.

325. The UK Government assessed that Iraq had failed to comply with a series of UN resolutions. Instead of disarming as these resolutions had demanded, Iraq was assessed to have concealed materials from past inspections and to have taken the opportunity of the absence of inspections to revive its WMD programmes.

326. In Section 4, the Inquiry has identified the importance of the ingrained belief of the Government and the intelligence community that Saddam Hussein's regime retained chemical and biological warfare capabilities, was determined to preserve and if possible enhance its capabilities, including at some point in the future a nuclear capability, and was pursuing an active and successful policy of deception and concealment.

327. This construct remained influential despite the lack of significant finds by inspectors in the period leading up to military action in March 2003, and even after the Occupation of Iraq.

328. Challenging Saddam Hussein's "claim" that he had no weapons of mass destruction, Mr Blair said in his speech on 18 March:

- "... we are asked to believe that after seven years of obstruction and non-compliance ... he [Saddam Hussein] voluntarily decided to do what he had consistently refused to do under coercion."
- "We are asked now seriously to accept that in the last few years – contrary to all history, contrary to all intelligence – Saddam decided unilaterally to destroy those weapons. I say that such a claim is palpably absurd."
- "... Iraq continues to deny that it has any weapons of mass destruction, although no serious intelligence service anywhere in the world believes it."
- "What is perfectly clear is that Saddam is playing the same old games in the same old way. Yes, there are minor concessions, but there has been no fundamental change of heart or mind."[154]

329. At no stage was the proposition that Iraq might no longer have chemical, biological or nuclear weapons or programmes identified and examined by either the JIC or the policy community.

---

[153] Public hearing, 20 July 2010, page 9.
[154] House of Commons, *Official Report*, 18 March 2003, columns 760-764.

330. Intelligence and assessments were used to prepare material to be used to support Government statements in a way which conveyed certainty without acknowledging the limitations of the intelligence.

331. Mr Blair's statement to the House of Commons on 18 March was the culmination of a series of public statements and interviews setting out the urgent need for the international community to act to bring about Iraq's disarmament in accordance with those resolutions, dating back to February 2002, before his meeting with President Bush at Crawford on 5 and 6 April.

332. As Mr Cook's resignation statement on 17 March made clear, it was possible for a Minister to draw different conclusions from the same information.

333. Mr Cook set out his doubts about Saddam Hussein's ability to deliver a strategic attack and the degree to which Iraq posed a "clear and present danger" to the UK. The points Mr Cook made included:

- "... neither the international community nor the British public is persuaded that there is an urgent and compelling reason for this military action in Iraq."

- "Over the past decade that strategy [of containment] had destroyed more weapons than in the Gulf War, dismantled Iraq's nuclear weapons programme and halted Saddam's medium and long range missile programmes."

- "Iraq probably has no weapons of mass destruction in the commonly understood sense of the term – namely a credible device capable of being delivered against a strategic city target. It probably ... has biological toxins and battlefield chemical munitions, but it has had them since the 1980s when US companies sold Saddam anthrax agents and the then British Government approved chemical and munitions factories. Why is it now so urgent that we should take military action to disarm a military capacity that has been there for twenty years, and which we helped to create? Why is it necessary to resort to war this week, while Saddam's ambition to complete his weapons programme is blocked by the presence of UN inspectors?"[155]

334. On 12 October 2004, announcing the withdrawal of two lines of intelligence reporting which had contributed to the pre-conflict judgements on mobile biological production facilities and the regime's intentions, Mr Straw stated that he did:

"... not accept, even with hindsight, that we were wrong to act as we did in the circumstances that we faced at the time. Even after reading all the evidence detailed by the Iraq Survey Group, it is still hard to believe that any regime could behave in so self-destructive a manner as to pretend that it had forbidden weaponry, when in fact it had not."[156]

---

[155] House of Commons, *Official Report*, 17 March 2003, columns 726-728.
[156] House of Commons, *Official Report*, 12 October 2004, columns 151-152.

335. Iraq had acted suspiciously over many years, which led to the inferences drawn by the Government and the intelligence community that it had been seeking to protect concealed WMD assets. When Iraq denied that it had retained any WMD capabilities, the UK Government accused it of lying.

336. This led the Government to emphasise the ability of Iraq successfully to deceive the inspectors, and cast doubt on the investigative capacity of the inspectors. The role of the inspectors, however, as was often pointed out, was not to seek out assets that had been hidden, but rather to validate Iraqi claims.

337. By March 2003, however:

- The Al Samoud 2 missiles which exceeded the range permitted by the UN, were being destroyed.
- The IAEA had concluded that there was no Iraqi nuclear programme of any significance.
- The inspectors believed that they were making progress and expected to achieve more co-operation from Iraq.
- The inspectors were preparing to step up their activities with U2 flights and interviews outside Iraq.

338. When the UK sought a further Security Council resolution in March 2003, the majority of the Council's members were not persuaded that the inspections process, and the diplomatic efforts surrounding it, had reached the end of the road. They did not agree that the time had come to terminate inspections and resort to force. The UK went to war without the explicit authorisation which it had sought from the Security Council.

339. At the time of the Parliamentary vote of 18 March, diplomatic options had not been exhausted. The point had not been reached where military action was the last resort.

The predicted increase in the threat to the UK as a result of military action in Iraq

340. Mr Blair had been advised that an invasion of Iraq was expected to increase the threat to the UK and UK interests from Al Qaida and its affiliates.

341. Asked about the risk that attacking Iraq with cruise missiles would "act as a recruiting sergeant for a young generation throughout the Islamic and Arab world", Mr Blair responded that:

> "... what was shocking about 11 September was not just the slaughter of innocent people but the knowledge that, had the terrorists been able, there would have been not 3,000 innocent dead, but 30,000 or 300,000 ... America did not attack the Al Qaida terrorist group ... [it] attacked America. They did not need to be

recruited ... Unless we take action against them, they will grow. That is why we should act."[157]

342. The JIC judged in October 2002 that "the greatest terrorist threat in the event of military action against Iraq will come from Al Qaida and other Islamic extremists"; and they would be "pursuing their own agenda".[158]

343. The JIC Assessment of 10 February 2003 repeated previous warnings that:

- Al Qaida and associated networks would remain the greatest terrorist threat to the UK and its activity would increase at the onset of any military action against Iraq.

- In the event of imminent regime collapse, Iraqi chemical and biological material could be transferred to terrorists, including Al Qaida.[159]

344. Addressing the prospects for the future, the JIC Assessment concluded:

"... **Al Qaida and associated groups will continue to represent by far the greatest terrorist threat to Western interests, and that threat will be heightened by military action against Iraq.** The broader threat from Islamist terrorists will also increase in the event of war, reflecting intensified anti-US/anti-Western sentiment in the Muslim world, including among Muslim communities in the West. And there is a risk that the transfer of CB [chemical and biological] material or expertise, during or in the aftermath of conflict, will enhance Al Qaida's capabilities."

345. In response to a call for Muslims everywhere to take up arms in defence of Iraq issued by Usama Bin Laden on 11 February, and a further call on 16 February for "compulsory jihad" by Muslims against the West, the JIC Assessment on 19 February predicted that the upward trend in the reports of threats to the UK was likely to continue.[160]

346. The JIC continued to warn in March that the threat from Al Qaida would increase at the onset of military action against Iraq.[161]

347. The JIC also warned that:

- Al Qaida activity in northern Iraq continued.

- Al Qaida might have established sleeper cells in Baghdad, to be activated during a US occupation.

---

[157] House of Commons, *Official Report*, 18 March 2003, column 769.
[158] JIC Assessment, 10 October 2002, 'International Terrorism: The Threat from Iraq'.
[159] JIC Assessment, 10 February 2003, 'International Terrorism: War with Iraq'.
[160] JIC Assessment, 19 February 2003, 'International Terrorism: The Current Threat from Islamic Extremists'.
[161] JIC Assessment, 12 March 2003, 'International Terrorism: War with Iraq: Update'.

348. The warning about the risk of chemical and biological weapons becoming available to extremist groups as a result of military action in Iraq was reiterated on 19 March.[162]

349. Addressing the JIC Assessment of 10 February 2003, Mr Blair told the Intelligence and Security Committee (ISC) later that year that:

"One of the most difficult aspects of this is that there was obviously a danger that in attacking Iraq you ended up provoking the very thing you were trying to avoid. On the other hand I think you had to ask the question, 'Could you really, as a result of that fear, leave the possibility that in time developed into a nexus between terrorism and WMD in an event?' This is where you've just got to make your judgement about this. But this is my judgement and it remains my judgement and I suppose time will tell whether it's true or it's not true."[163]

350. In its response to the ISC Report, the Government drew:

"... attention to the difficult judgement that had to be made and the factors on both sides of the argument to be taken into account."[164]

351. Baroness Manningham-Buller told the Inquiry:

"By 2003/2004 we were receiving an increasing number of leads to terrorist activity from within the UK ... our involvement in Iraq radicalised, for want of a better word ... a few among a generation ... [who] saw our involvement in Iraq, on top of our involvement in Afghanistan, as being an attack on Islam."[165]

352. Asked about the proposition that it was right to remove Saddam Hussein's regime to forestall a fusion of weapons of mass destruction and international terrorism at some point in the future, and if it had eliminated a threat of terrorism from his regime, Baroness Manningham-Buller replied:

"It eliminated the threat of terrorism from his direct regime; it didn't eliminate the threat of terrorism using unconventional methods ... So using weapons of mass destruction as a terrorist weapon is still a potential threat.

"After all Usama Bin Laden said it was the duty of members of his organisation or those in sympathy with it to acquire and use these weapons. It is interesting that ... such efforts as we have seen to get access to these sort of materials have been low-grade and not very professional, but it must be a cause of concern to my former colleagues that at some stage terrorist groups will resort to these methods.

---

[162] Note JIC, 19 March 2003, 'Saddam: The Beginning of the End'.
[163] Intelligence and Security Committee, *Iraqi Weapons of Mass Destruction – Intelligence and Assessments*, September 2003, Cm5972, paragraph 128.
[164] *Government Response to the Intelligence and Security Committee Report on Iraqi Weapons of Mass Destruction – Intelligence and Assessments, 11 September 2003*, February 2004, Cm6118, paragraph 22.
[165] Public hearing, 20 July 2010, page 19.

In that respect, I don't think toppling Saddam Hussein is germane to the long-term ambitions of some terrorist groups to use them."[166]

353. Asked specifically about the theory that at some point in the future Saddam Hussein would probably have brought together international terrorism and weapons of mass destruction in a threat to Western interests, Baroness Manningham-Buller responded:

"It is a hypothetical theory. It certainly wasn't of concern in either the short-term or the medium-term to my colleagues and myself."[167]

354. Asked if "a war in Iraq would aggravate the threat from whatever source to the United Kingdom", Baroness Manningham-Buller stated that that was the view communicated by the JIC Assessments.[168]

355. Baroness Manningham-Buller subsequently added that if Ministers had read the JIC Assessments they could "have had no doubt" about that risk.[169] She said that by the time of the July 2005 attacks in London:

"... an increasing number of British-born individuals ... were attracted to the ideology of Usama Bin Laden and saw the West's activities in Iraq and Afghanistan as threatening their fellow religionists and the Muslim world."

356. Asked whether the judgement that the effect of the invasion of Iraq had increased the terrorist threat to the UK was based on hard evidence or a broader assessment, Baroness Manningham-Buller replied:

"I think we can produce evidence because of the numerical evidence of the number of plots, the number of leads, the number of people identified, and the correlation of that to Iraq and statements of people as to why they were involved ... So I think the answer to your ... question: yes."[170]

357. In its request for a statement, the Inquiry asked Mr Blair if he had read the JIC Assessment of 10 February 2002, and what weight he had given to it when he decided to take military action.[171]

358. In his statement Mr Blair wrote:

"I was aware of the JIC Assessment of 10 February that the Al Qaida threat to the UK would increase. But I took the view then and take the same view now that to have backed down because of the threat of terrorism would be completely wrong.

[166] Public hearing, 20 July 2010, pages 23-24.
[167] Public hearing, 20 July 2010, page 24.
[168] Public hearing, 20 July 2010, page 31.
[169] Public hearing, 20 July 2010, page 33.
[170] Public hearing, 20 July 2010, pages 33-34.
[171] Inquiry request for a witness statement, 13 December 2010, Qs 11c and 11d page 7.

In any event, following 9/11 and Afghanistan we were a terrorist target and, as recent events in Europe and the US show, irrespective of Iraq, there are ample justifications such terrorists will use as excuses for terrorism."[172]

The UK's relationship with the US

359. The UK's relationship with the US was a determining factor in the Government's decisions over Iraq.

360. It was the US Administration which decided in late 2001 to make dealing with the problem of Saddam Hussein's regime the second priority, after the ousting of the Taliban in Afghanistan, in the "Global War on Terror". In that period, the US Administration turned against a strategy of continued containment of Iraq, which it was pursuing before the 9/11 attacks.

361. This was not, initially, the view of the UK Government. Its stated view at that time was that containment had been broadly effective, and that it could be adapted in order to remain sustainable. Containment continued to be the declared policy of the UK throughout the first half of 2002.

362. The declared objectives of the UK and the US towards Iraq up to the time of the invasion differed. The US was explicitly seeking to achieve a change of regime; the UK to achieve the disarmament of Iraq, as required by UN Security Council resolutions.

363. Most crucially, the US Administration committed itself to a timetable for military action which did not align with, and eventually overrode, the timetable and processes for inspections in Iraq which had been set by the UN Security Council. The UK wanted UNMOVIC and the IAEA to have time to complete their work, and wanted the support of the Security Council, and of the international community more widely, before any further steps were taken. This option was foreclosed by the US decision.

364. On these and other important points, including the planning for the post-conflict period and the functioning of the Coalition Provisional Authority (CPA), the UK Government decided that it was right or necessary to defer to its close ally and senior partner, the US.

365. It did so essentially for two reasons:

- Concern that vital areas of co-operation between the UK and the US could be damaged if the UK did not give the US its full support over Iraq.
- The belief that the best way to influence US policy towards the direction preferred by the UK was to commit full and unqualified support, and seek to persuade from the inside.

---

[172] Statement, 14 January 2011, page 16.

366. The UK Government was right to think very carefully about both of those points.

367. First, the close strategic alliance with the US has been a cornerstone of the UK's foreign and security policy under successive governments since the Second World War. Mr Blair rightly attached great importance to preserving and strengthening it.

368. After the attacks on the US on 11 September 2001, that relationship was reinforced when Mr Blair declared that the UK would stand "shoulder to shoulder" with the US to defeat and eradicate international terrorism.[173] The action that followed in Afghanistan to bring about the fall of the Taliban served to strengthen and deepen the sense of shared endeavour.

369. When the US Administration turned its attention to regime change in Iraq as part of the second phase of the "Global War on Terror", Mr Blair's immediate response was to seek to offer a partnership and to work with it to build international support for the position that Iraq was a threat which had to be dealt with.

370. In Mr Blair's view, the decision to stand alongside the US was in the UK's long-term national interests. In his speech of 18 March 2003, he argued that the handling of Iraq would:

"... determine the way in which Britain and the world confront the central security threat of the 21st century, the development of the United Nations, the relationship between Europe and the United States, the relations within the European Union and the way in which the United States engages with the rest of the world. So it could hardly be more important. It will determine the pattern of international politics for the next generation."

371. In his memoir in 2010, Mr Blair wrote:

"I knew in the final analysis I would be with the US, because it was right morally and strategically. But we should make a last ditch attempt for a peaceful solution. First to make the moral case for removing Saddam ... Second, to try one more time to reunite the international community behind a clear base for action in the event of a continuing breach."[174]

372. Concern about the consequences, were the UK not to give full support to the US, featured prominently in policy calculations across Whitehall. Mr Hoon, for example, sought advice from Sir Kevin Tebbit, MOD Permanent Under Secretary, on the implications for the alliance of the UK's approach to Iraq.[175]

373. Although there has historically been a very close relationship between the British and American peoples and a close identity of values between our democracies, it is an

---

[173] The National Archives, 11 September 2001, *September 11 attacks: Prime Minister's statement.*
[174] Blair T. *A Journey.* Hutchinson, 2010.
[175] Minute Tebbit to Secretary of State [MOD], 14 January 2003, 'Iraq: What If?'.

alliance founded not on emotion, but on a hard-headed appreciation of mutual benefit. The benefits do not by any means flow only in one direction.

374. In his memoir, Mr Blair wrote:

"... I agreed with the basic US analysis of Saddam as a threat; I thought he was a monster; and to break the US partnership in such circumstances, when America's key allies were all rallying round, would in my view, then (and now) have done major long-term damage to that relationship."

375. The Government was right to weigh the possible consequences for the wider alliance with the US very carefully, as previous Governments have done. A policy of direct opposition to the US would have done serious short-term damage to the relationship, but it is questionable whether it would have broken the partnership.

376. Over the past seven decades, the UK and US have adopted differing, and sometimes conflicting, positions on major issues, for example Suez, the Vietnam War, the Falklands, Grenada, Bosnia, the Arab/Israel dispute and, at times, Northern Ireland. Those differences did not fundamentally call into question the practice of close co-operation, to mutual advantage, on the overall relationship, including defence and intelligence.

377. The opposition of Germany and France to US policy in 2002 to 2003 does not appear to have had a lasting impact on the relationships of those countries with the US, despite the bitterness at the time.

378. However, a decision not to oppose does not have to be translated into unqualified support. Throughout the post-Second World War period (and, notably, during the wartime alliance), the UK's relationship with the US and the commonality of interests therein have proved strong enough to bear the weight of different approaches to international problems and not infrequent disagreements.

379. Had the UK stood by its differing position on Iraq – which was not an opposed position, but one in which the UK had identified conditions seen as vital by the UK Government – the Inquiry does not consider that this would have led to a fundamental or lasting change in the UK's relationship with the US.

380. This is a matter of judgement, and one on which Mr Blair, bearing the responsibility of leadership, took a different view.

381. The second reason for committing unqualified support was, by standing alongside and taking part in the planning, the UK would be able to influence US policy.

382. Mr Blair's stalwart support for the US after 9/11 had a significant impact in that country. Mr Blair developed a close working relationship with President Bush. He used this to compare notes and inject his views on the major issues of the day, and it is clear from the records of the discussions that President Bush encouraged that dialogue and listened to Mr Blair's opinions.

383. Mr Blair expressed his views in frequent telephone calls and in meetings with the President. There was also a very active channel between his Foreign Affairs Adviser and the President's National Security Advisor. Mr Blair also sent detailed written Notes to the President.

384. Mr Jonathan Powell, Mr Blair's Chief of Staff, told the Inquiry:

"... the Prime Minister had a habit of writing notes, both internally and to President Clinton and to President Bush, on all sorts of subjects, because he found it better to put something in writing rather than to simply talk about it orally and get it much more concretely ... in focused terms."[176]

385. Mr Blair drew on information and briefing received from Whitehall departments, but evidently drafted many or most of his Notes to the President himself, showing the drafts to his close advisers in No.10 but not (ahead of despatch) to the relevant Cabinet Ministers.

386. How best to exercise influence with the President of the United States is a matter for the tactical judgement of the Prime Minister, and will vary between Prime Ministers and Presidents. In relation to Iraq, Mr Blair's judgement, as he and others have explained, was that objectives the UK identified for a successful strategy should not be expressed as conditions for its support.

387. Mr Powell told the Inquiry that Mr Blair was offering the US a "partnership to try to get to a wide coalition" and "setting out a framework" and to try to persuade the US to move in a particular direction.[177]

388. Mr Blair undoubtedly influenced the President's decision to go to the UN Security Council in the autumn of 2002. On other critical decisions set out in the Report, he did not succeed in changing the approach determined in Washington.

389. This issue is addressed in the Lessons section of this Executive Summary, under the heading "The decision to go to war".

Decision-making

390. The way in which the policy on Iraq was developed and decisions were taken and implemented within the UK Government has been at the heart of the Inquiry's work and fundamental to its conclusions.

391. The Inquiry has set out in Section 2 of the Report the roles and responsibilities of key individuals and bodies in order to assist the reader. It is also publishing with the Report many of the documents which illuminate who took the key decisions and on what

---

[176] Public hearing, 18 January 2010, page 38.
[177] Public hearing, 18 January 2010, pages 77-78.

basis, including the full record of the discussion on Iraq in Cabinet on five key occasions pre-conflict, and policy advice to Ministers which is not normally disclosed.

Collective responsibility

392. Under UK constitutional conventions – in which the Prime Minister leads the Government – Cabinet is the main mechanism by which the most senior members of the Government take collective responsibility for its most important decisions. Cabinet is supported by a system of Ministerial Committees whose role is to identify, test and develop policy options; analyse and mitigate risks; and debate and hone policy proposals until they are endorsed across the Government.[178]

393. The *Ministerial Code* in place in 2003 said:

"The Cabinet is supported by Ministerial Committees (both standing and ad hoc) which have a two-fold purpose. First, they relieve the pressure on the Cabinet itself by settling as much business as possible at a lower level or, failing that, by clarifying the issues and defining the points of disagreement. Second, they support the principle of collective responsibility by ensuring that, even though an important question may never reach the Cabinet itself, the decision will be fully considered and the final judgement will be sufficiently authoritative to ensure that the Government as a whole can properly be expected to accept responsibility for it."[179]

394. The Code also said:

"The business of the Cabinet and Ministerial Committees consists in the main of:

    a.   questions which significantly engage the collective responsibility of the Government because they raise major issues of policy or because they are of critical importance to the public;

    b.   questions on which there is an unresolved argument between Departments."

395. Lord Wilson of Dinton told the Inquiry that between January 1998 and January 1999, in the run-up to and immediate aftermath of Operation Desert Fox in December 1998 (see Section 1.1), as Cabinet Secretary, he had attended and noted 21 Ministerial discussions on Iraq: 10 in Cabinet, of which seven had "some substance"; five in DOP; and six ad hoc meetings, including one JIC briefing.[180] Discussions in Cabinet or a Cabinet Committee would have been supported by the relevant part of the Cabinet Secretariat, the Overseas and Defence Secretariat (OD Sec).

---

[178] *Ministerial Code*, 2001, page 3.
[179] *Ministerial Code*, 2001, page 3.
[180] Public hearing, 25 January 2011, page 11.

396. Similarly, Lord Wilson stated that, between 11 September 2001 and January 2002, the Government's response to international terrorism and the subsequent military action against the Taliban in Afghanistan had been managed through 46 Ministerial meetings.[181]

397. The last meeting of DOP on Iraq before the 2003 conflict, however, took place in March 1999.[182]

398. In April 2002, the MOD clearly expected consideration of military options to be addressed through DOP. Mr Simon Webb, the MOD Policy Director, advised Mr Hoon that:

> "Even these preparatory steps would properly need a Cabinet Committee decision, based on a minute from the Defence Secretary ..."[183]

399. Most decisions on Iraq pre-conflict were taken either bilaterally between Mr Blair and the relevant Secretary of State or in meetings between Mr Blair, Mr Straw and Mr Hoon, with No.10 officials and, as appropriate, Mr John Scarlett (Chairman of the JIC), Sir Richard Dearlove and Adm Boyce. Some of those meetings were minuted; some were not.

400. As the guidance for the Cabinet Secretariat makes clear, the purpose of the minute of a meeting is to set out the conclusions reached so that those who have to take action know precisely what to do; the second purpose is to "give the reasons why the conclusions were reached".[184]

401. Lord Turnbull, Cabinet Secretary from 2002 to 2005, described Mr Blair's characteristic way of working with his Cabinet colleagues as:

> "... 'I like to move fast. I don't want to spend a lot of time in kind of conflict resolution, and, therefore, I will get the people who will make this thing move quickly and efficiently.' That was his sort of characteristic style, but it has drawbacks."[185]

402. Lord Turnbull subsequently told the Inquiry that the group described above was "a professional forum ... they had ... with one possible exception [Ms Clare Short, the International Development Secretary], the right people in the room. It wasn't the kind of sofa government in the sense of the Prime Minister and his special advisers and political cronies".[186]

---

[181] Public hearing, 25 January 2011, page 11.
[182] Email Cabinet Office to Secretary Iraq Inquiry, 5 July 2011, 'FOI request for joint MOD/FCO memo on Iraq Policy 1999'.
[183] Minute Webb to PS/Secretary of State, 12 April 2002, 'Bush and the War on Terrorism'.
[184] Cabinet Office, June 2001, *Guide to Minute Taking*.
[185] Public hearing, 13 January 2010, page 28.
[186] Public hearing, 13 January 2010, pages 45-46.

403. In July 2004, Lord Butler's Report stated that his Committee was:

"... concerned that the informality and circumscribed character of the Government's procedures which we saw in the context of policy-making towards Iraq risks reducing the scope for informed collective political judgement. Such risks are particularly significant in a field like the subject of our Review, where hard facts are inherently difficult to come by and the quality of judgement is accordingly all the more important."[187]

404. In response, Mr Blair agreed that:

"... where a small group is brought together to work on operational military planning and developing the diplomatic strategy, in future such a group will operate formally as an ad hoc Cabinet Committee."[188]

405. The Inquiry considers that where policy options include significant military deployments, particularly where they will have implications for the responsibilities of more than one Cabinet Minister, are likely to be controversial, and/or are likely to give rise to significant risks, the options should be considered by a group of Ministers meeting regularly, whether or not they are formally designated as a Cabinet Committee, so that Cabinet as a whole can be enabled to take informed collective decisions.

406. Describing the important function a Cabinet Committee can play, Mr Powell wrote:

"Most of the important decisions of the Blair Government were taken either in informal meetings of Ministers and officials or by Cabinet Committees ... Unlike the full Cabinet, a Cabinet Committee has the right people present, including, for example, the military Chiefs of Staff or scientific advisers, its members are well briefed, it can take as long as it likes over its discussion on the basis of well-prepared papers, and it is independently chaired by a senior Minister with no departmental vested interest."[189]

407. The Inquiry concurs with this description of the function of a Cabinet Committee when it is working well. In particular, it recognises the important function which a Minister without departmental responsibilities for the issues under consideration can play. This can provide some external challenge from experienced members of the government and mitigate any tendency towards group-think. In the case of Iraq, for example, the inclusion of the Chancellor of the Exchequer or Deputy Prime Minister, as senior members of the Cabinet, or of Mr Cook, as a former Foreign Secretary known to have concerns about the policy, could have provided an element of challenge.

---

[187] *Review of Intelligence on Weapons of Mass Destruction* ["The Butler Report"], 14 July 2004, HC 898.
[188] Cabinet Office, *Review on Intelligence on Weapons of Mass Destruction: Implementation of its Conclusions*, March 2005, Cm6492.
[189] Powell J. *The New Machiavelli: How to wield power in the modern world.* The Bodley Head, 2010.

408. Mr Powell likewise recognises the importance of having written advice which can be seen before a meeting, allowing all those present to have shared information and the opportunity to digest it and seek further advice if necessary. This allows the time in meetings to be used productively.

409. The Inquiry considers that there should have been collective discussion by a Cabinet Committee or small group of Ministers on the basis of inter-departmental advice agreed at a senior level between officials at a number of decision points which had a major impact on the development of UK policy before the invasion of Iraq. Those were:

- The decision at the beginning of December 2001 to offer to work with President Bush on a strategy to deal with Iraq as part of Phase 2 of the "War on Terror", despite the fact that there was no evidence of any Iraqi involvement with the attacks on the US or active links to Al Qaida.

- The adoption of the position at the end of February 2002 that Iraq was a threat which had to be dealt with, together with the assumption that the only certain means to remove Saddam Hussein and his regime was to invade Iraq and impose a new government.

- The position Mr Blair should adopt in discussions with President Bush at Crawford in April 2002. The meeting at Chequers on 2 April was given a presentation on the military options and did not explore the political and legal implications of a conflict with Iraq. There was no FCO representative at the Chequers meeting and no subsequent meeting with Mr Straw and Mr Hoon.

- The position Mr Blair should adopt in his discussion with President Bush at Camp David on 5 and 6 September 2002. Mr Blair's long Note of 28 July, telling President Bush "I will be with you, whatever", was seen, before it was sent, only by No.10 officials. A copy was sent afterwards to Mr Straw, but not to Mr Hoon. While the Note was marked "Personal" (to signal that it should have a restricted circulation), it represented an extensive statement of the UK Government's position by the Prime Minister to the President of the United States. The Foreign and Defence Secretaries should certainly have been given an opportunity to comment on the draft in advance.

- A discussion in mid-September 2002 on the need for robust post-conflict planning.

- The decision on 31 October 2002 to offer ground forces to the US for planning purposes.

- The decision on 17 January 2003 to deploy large scale ground forces for operations in southern Iraq.

- The position Mr Blair should adopt in his discussion with President Bush in Washington on 31 January 2003.

- The proposals in Mr Blair's Note to President Bush of 19 February suggesting a deadline for a vote in the Security Council of 14 March.

- A review of UK policy at the end of February 2003 when the inspectors had found no evidence of WMD and there was only limited support for the second resolution in the Security Council.

- The question of whether Iraq had committed further material breaches as specified in operative paragraph 4 of resolution 1441 (2002), as posed in Mr Brummell's letter of 14 March to Mr Rycroft.

410. In addition to providing a mechanism to probe and challenge the implications of proposals before decisions were taken, a Cabinet Committee or a more structured process might have identified some of the wider implications and risks associated with the deployment of military forces to Iraq. It might also have offered the opportunity to remedy some of the deficiencies in planning which are identified in Section 6 of the Report. There will, of course, be other policy issues which would benefit from the same approach.

411. Cabinet has a different role to that of a Cabinet Committee.

412. Mr Powell has written that:

"... Cabinet is the right place to ratify decisions, the right place for people to raise concerns if they have not done so before, the right place for briefings by the Prime Minister and other Ministers on strategic issues, the right place to ensure political unity; but it is categorically not the right place for an informed decision on difficult and detailed policy issues."[190]

413. In 2009, in a statement explaining a Cabinet decision to veto the release of minutes of one of its meetings under the Freedom of Information Act 2000, Mr Straw explained the need for frank discussion at Cabinet very cogently:

"Serious and controversial decisions must be taken with free, frank – even blunt deliberations between colleagues. Dialogue must be fearless. Ministers must have the confidence to challenge each other in private. They must ensure that decisions have been properly thought through, sounding out all possibilities before committing themselves to a course of action. They must not feel inhibited from advancing options that may be unpopular or controversial. They must not be deflected from expressing dissent by the fear that they may be held personally to account for views that are later cast aside."[191]

---

[190] Powell J. *The New Machiavelli: How to wield power in the modern world.* The Bodley Head, 2010.
[191] Statement J Straw, 23 February 2009, 'Exercise of the Executive Override under section 53 of the Freedom of Information Act 2000 in respect of the decision of the Information Commissioner dated 18 February 2008 (Ref: FS50165372) as upheld by the decision of the Information Tribunal of 27 January 2009 (Ref: EA/2008/0024 and EA/2008/0029): Statement of Reasons'.

414. Mr Blair told the Inquiry that:

"... the discussion that we had in Cabinet was substantive discussion. We had it again and again and again, and the options were very simple. The options were: a sanctions framework that was effective; alternatively, the UN inspectors doing the job, alternatively, you have to remove Saddam. Those were the options."[192]

415. Mr Blair added:

"Nobody in the Cabinet was unaware of ... what the whole issue was about. It was the thing running throughout the whole of the political mainstream at the time. There were members of the Cabinet who would challenge and disagree, but most of them agreed."[193]

416. The Inquiry has seen the minutes of 26 meetings of Cabinet between 28 February 2002 and 17 March 2003 at which Iraq was mentioned and Cabinet Secretariat notebooks. Cabinet was certainly given updates on diplomatic developments and had opportunities to discuss the general issues. The number of occasions on which there was a substantive discussion of the policy was very much more limited.

417. There were substantive discussions of the policy on Iraq, although not necessarily of all the issues (as the Report sets out), in Cabinet on 7 March and 23 September 2002 and 16 January, 13 March and 17 March 2003. Those are the records which are being published with the Report.

418. At the Cabinet meeting on 7 March 2002, Mr Blair concluded:

"... the concerns expressed in discussion were justified. It was important that the United States did not appear to be acting unilaterally. It was critically important to reinvigorate the Middle East Peace Process. Any military action taken against President Saddam Hussein's regime had to be effective. On the other hand, the Iraqi regime was in clear breach of its obligations under several United Nations Security Council resolutions. Its WMD programmes posed a threat to peace. Iraq's neighbours regarded President Saddam Hussein as a danger. The right strategy was to engage closely with the Government of the United States in order to be in a position to shape policy and its presentation. The international community should proceed in a measured but determined way to decide how to respond to the real threat represented by the Iraqi regime. No decisions to launch military action had been taken and any action taken would be in accordance with international law.

"The Cabinet, 'Took note, with approval.'"[194]

---

[192] Public hearing, 29 January 2010, page 22.
[193] Public hearing, 29 January 2010, pages 228-229.
[194] Cabinet Conclusions, 7 March 2002.

419. Cabinet on 17 March 2003 noted Mr Blair's conclusion that "the diplomatic process was at an end; Saddam Hussein would be given an ultimatum to leave Iraq; and the House of Commons would be asked to endorse the use of military action against Iraq to enforce compliance, if necessary".

420. In Section 5 of the Report, the Inquiry concludes that Lord Goldsmith should have been asked to provide written advice which fully reflected the position on 17 March and explained the legal basis on which the UK could take military action and set out the risks of legal challenge.

421. There was no substantive discussion of the military options, despite promises by Mr Blair, before the meeting on 17 March.

422. In his statement for the Inquiry, Mr Hoon wrote that by the time he joined Cabinet, in 1999:

"... the pattern of the organisation and format of Cabinet meetings was ... well established. Tony Blair was well known to be extremely concerned about leaks from Cabinet discussions ... It was my perception that, largely as a consequence of this, he did not normally expect key decisions to be made in the course of Cabinet meetings. Papers were submitted to the Cabinet Office, and in turn by the Cabinet Office to appropriate Cabinet Committees for decisions."[195]

423. Mr Hoon wrote:

"At no time when I was serving in the Ministry of Defence were other Cabinet Ministers involved in discussions about the deployment of specific forces and the nature of their operations. Relevant details would have been circulated to 10 Downing Street or other Government departments as necessary ... I do not recall a single Cabinet level discussion of specific troop deployments and the nature of their operations."[196]

424. The Inquiry recognises that there will be operational constraints on discussion of the details of military deployments, but that would not preclude the discussion of the principles and the implications of military options.

425. In January 2006, the Cabinet discussed the proposal to deploy military forces to Helmand later that year.

426. The Inquiry also recognises that the nature of foreign policy, as the Report vividly demonstrates, requires the Prime Minister of the UK, the Foreign Secretary and their most senior officials to be involved in negotiating and agreeing policy on a day-by-day, and sometimes hour-by-hour basis.

---

[195] Statement, 2 April 2015, page 1.
[196] Statement, 2 April 2015, page 2.

427. It would neither be necessary nor feasible to seek a mandate from Cabinet at each stage of a discussion. That reinforces the importance of ensuring Cabinet is kept informed as strategy evolves, is given the opportunity to raise questions and is asked to endorse key decisions. Cabinet Ministers need more information than will be available from the media, especially on sensitive issues of foreign and security policy.

428. In 2009, three former Cabinet Secretaries[197] told the House of Lords Select Committee on the Constitution:

> "... each of us, as Secretary of the Cabinet, has been constantly conscious of his responsibility to the Cabinet collectively and of the need to have regard to the needs and responsibilities of the other members of the Cabinet (and indeed of other Ministers) as well of those of the Prime Minister. That has coloured our relationships with Number 10 as well as those with other Ministers and their departments."[198]

429. Lord Turnbull told the Inquiry that Mr Blair:

> "... wanted a step change in the work on delivery and reform, which I hope I managed to give him. Now ... how does the Cabinet Secretary work? You come in and you are – even with the two roles that you have, head of an organisation of half a million civil servants and in some sense co-ordinating a public sector of about five million people. You have to make choices as to where you make your effort, and I think the policy I followed was not to take an issue over from someone to whom it was delegated simply because it was big and important, but you have to make a judgement as to whether it is being handled competently, whether that particular part is, in a sense, under pressure, whether you think they are getting it wrong in some sense, or they are missing certain important things."[199]

430. The responsibility of the Cabinet Secretary to ensure that members of Cabinet are fully engaged in ways that allow them to accept collective responsibility and to meet their departmental obligations nevertheless remains.

Advice on the legal basis for military action

431. The Inquiry has reviewed the debate that took place within the Government and how it reached its decision.

432. The circumstances in which it was ultimately decided that there was a legal basis for UK participation were far from satisfactory.

433. It was not until 13 March 2003 that Lord Goldsmith advised that there was, on balance, a secure legal basis for military action.

---

[197] Lord Armstrong of Ilminster, Lord Butler of Brockwell and Lord Wilson of Dinton.
[198] Fourth Report from the House of Lords Select Committee on the Constitution, Session 2009-10, *The Cabinet Office and the Centre of Government*, HL Paper 30.
[199] Public hearing, 13 January 2010, page 3.

434. In the letter of 14 March 2003 from Lord Goldsmith's office to No.10, which is addressed in Section 5 of the Report, Mr Blair was told that an essential ingredient of the legal basis was that he, himself, should be satisfied of the fact that Iraq was in breach of resolution 1441.

435. In accordance with that advice, it was Mr Blair who decided that, so far as the UK was concerned, Iraq was and remained in breach of resolution 1441.

436. Apart from No.10's response to the letter of 14 March, sent the following day, in terms that can only be described as perfunctory, no formal record was made of that decision and the precise grounds on which it was made remain unclear.

437. The Inquiry was told, and it accepts, that it would have been possible at that stage for the UK Government to have decided not to go ahead with military action if it had been necessary to make a decision to do so; or if the House of Commons on 18 March had voted against the Government.

438. Although, when resolution 1441 was adopted, there was unanimous support for a rigorous inspections and monitoring regime backed by the threat of military force as the means to disarm Iraq, there was no such consensus in the Security Council in March 2003. If the matter had been left to the Security Council to decide, military action might have been postponed and, possibly, avoided.

439. The Charter of the United Nations vests responsibility for the maintenance of peace and security in the Security Council. The UK Government was claiming to act on behalf of the international community "to uphold the authority of the Security Council", knowing that it did not have a majority in the Security Council in support of its actions. In those circumstances, the UK's actions undermined the authority of the Security Council.

440. A determination by the Security Council on whether Iraq was in fact in material breach of resolution 1441 would have furthered the UK's aspiration to uphold the authority of the Council.

The timing of Lord Goldsmith's advice on the interpretation of resolution 1441

441. Following the adoption of resolution 1441, a decision was taken to delay the receipt of formal advice from Lord Goldsmith.

442. On 11 November 2002, Mr Powell told Lord Goldsmith that there should be a meeting some time before Christmas to discuss the legal position.

443. On 9 December, formal "instructions" to provide advice were sent to Lord Goldsmith. They were sent by the FCO on behalf of the FCO and the MOD as well as No.10.

444. The instructions made it clear that Lord Goldsmith should not provide an immediate response.

445. When Lord Goldsmith met Mr Powell, Sir David Manning and Baroness Morgan (Director of Political and Government Relations to the Prime Minister) on 19 December, he was told that he was not, at that stage, being asked for his advice; and that, when he was, it would be helpful for him to discuss a draft with Mr Blair in the first instance.

446. Until 7 March 2003, Mr Blair and Mr Powell asked that Lord Goldsmith's views on the legal effect of resolution 1441 should be tightly held and not shared with Ministerial colleagues without No.10's permission.

447. Lord Goldsmith agreed that approach.

448. Lord Goldsmith provided draft advice to Mr Blair on 14 January 2003. As instructed he did not, at that time, provide a copy of his advice to Mr Straw or to Mr Hoon.

449. Although Lord Goldsmith was invited to attend Cabinet on 16 January, there was no discussion of Lord Goldsmith's views.

450. Mr Straw was aware, in general terms, of Lord Goldsmith's position but he was not provided with a copy of Lord Goldsmith's draft advice before Cabinet on 16 January. He did not read it until at least two weeks later.

451. The draft advice of 14 January should have been provided to Mr Straw, Mr Hoon and the Cabinet Secretary, all of whose responsibilities were directly engaged.

452. Lord Goldsmith provided Mr Blair with further advice on 30 January. It was not seen by anyone outside No.10.

453. Lord Goldsmith discussed the negotiating history of resolution 1441 with Mr Straw, Sir Jeremy Greenstock, with White House officials and the State Department's Legal Advisers. They argued that resolution 1441 could be interpreted as not requiring a second resolution. The US Government's position was that it would not have agreed to resolution 1441 had its terms required one.

454. When Lord Goldsmith met No.10 officials on 27 February, he told them that he had reached the view that a "reasonable case" could be made that resolution 1441 was capable of reviving the authorisation to use force in resolution 678 (1990) without a further resolution, if there were strong factual grounds for concluding that Iraq had failed to take the final opportunity offered by resolution 1441.

455. Until that time, No.10 could not have been sure that Lord Goldsmith would advise that there was a basis on which military action against Iraq could be taken in the absence of a further decision of the Security Council.

456. In the absence of Lord Goldsmith's formal advice, uncertainties about the circumstances in which the UK would be able to participate in military action continued, although the possibility of a second resolution remained.

457. Lord Goldsmith provided formal written advice on 7 March.

Lord Goldsmith's advice of 7 March 2003

458. Lord Goldsmith's formal advice of 7 March set out alternative interpretations of the legal effect of resolution 1441. He concluded that the safer route would be to seek a second resolution, and he set out the ways in which, in the absence of a second resolution, the matter might be brought before a court. Lord Goldsmith identified a key question to be whether or not there was a need for an assessment of whether Iraq's conduct constituted a failure to take the final opportunity or a failure fully to co-operate within the meaning of operative paragraph 4, such that the basis of the cease-fire was destroyed.

459. Lord Goldsmith wrote (paragraph 26): "A narrow textual reading of the resolution suggested no such assessment was needed because the Security Council had pre-determined the issue. Public statements, on the other hand, say otherwise."

460. While Lord Goldsmith remained "of the opinion that the safest legal course would be to secure a second resolution", he concluded (paragraph 28) that "a reasonable case can be made that resolution 1441 was capable of reviving the authorisation in resolution 678 without a further resolution".

461. Lord Goldsmith wrote that a reasonable case did not mean that, if the matter ever came to court, he would be confident that the court would agree with this view. He judged a court might well conclude that OPs 4 and 12 required a further Security Council decision in order to revive the authorisation in resolution 678.

462. Lord Goldsmith noted that on a number of previous occasions, including in relation to Operation Desert Fox in Iraq in 1998 and Kosovo in 1999, UK forces had participated in military action on the basis of advice from previous Attorneys General that (paragraph 30) "the legality of the action under international law was no more than reasonably arguable".

463. Lord Goldsmith warned Mr Blair (paragraph 29):

> "... the argument that resolution 1441 alone has revived the authorisation to use force in resolution 678 will only be sustainable if there are strong factual grounds for concluding that Iraq failed to take the final opportunity. In other words, we would need to be able to demonstrate hard evidence of non-compliance and non-co-operation ... the views of UNMOVIC and the IAEA will be highly significant in this respect."

464. Lord Goldsmith added:

"In the light of the latest reporting by UNMOVIC, you will need to consider extremely carefully whether the evidence of non-co-operation and non-compliance by Iraq is sufficiently compelling to justify the conclusion that Iraq has failed to take its final opportunity."

465. Mr Straw, Mr Hoon, Dr John Reid (Minister without Portfolio and Labour Party Chair) and the Chiefs of Staff had all seen Lord Goldsmith's advice of 7 March before the No.10 meeting on 11 March, but it is not clear how and when it reached them.

466. Other Ministers whose responsibilities were directly engaged, including Mr Gordon Brown (Chancellor of the Exchequer) and Ms Short, and their senior officials, did not see the advice.

Lord Goldsmith's arrival at a "better view"

467. At the meeting on 11 March, Mr Blair stated that Lord Goldsmith's "advice made it clear that a reasonable case could be made" that resolution 1441 was "capable of reviving" the authorisation of resolution 678, "although of course a second resolution would be preferable". There was concern, however, that the advice did not offer a clear indication that military action would be lawful.

468. Lord Goldsmith was asked, after the meeting, by Adm Boyce on behalf of the Armed Forces, and by the Treasury Solicitor, Ms Juliet Wheldon, in respect of the Civil Service, to give a clear-cut answer on whether military action would be lawful rather than unlawful.

469. On 12 March, Mr Blair and Mr Straw reached the view that there was no chance of securing a majority in the Security Council in support of the draft resolution of 7 March and there was a risk of one or more vetoes if the resolution was put to a vote.

470. There is no evidence to indicate that Lord Goldsmith was informed of their conclusion.

471. Lord Goldsmith concluded on 13 March that, on balance, the "better view" was that the conditions for the operation of the revival argument were met in this case, meaning that there was a lawful basis for the use of force without a further resolution beyond resolution 1441.

The exchange of letters on 14 and 15 March 2003

472. Mr David Brummell (Legal Secretary to the Law Officers) wrote to Mr Matthew Rycroft (Mr Blair's Private Secretary for Foreign Affairs) on 14 March:

"It is an essential part of the legal basis for military action without a further resolution of the Security Council that there is strong evidence that Iraq has failed to comply with and co-operate fully in the implementation of resolution 1441 and has thus failed to take the final opportunity offered by the Security Council in that resolution. The Attorney General understands that it is unequivocally the Prime Minister's view that Iraq has committed further material breaches as specified in [operative] paragraph 4 of resolution 1441, but as this is a judgement for the Prime Minister, the Attorney would be grateful for confirmation that this is the case."

473. Mr Rycroft replied to Mr Brummell on 15 March:

"This is to confirm that it is indeed the Prime Minister's unequivocal view that Iraq is in further material breach of its obligations, as in OP4 of UNSCR 1441, because of 'false statements or omissions in the declarations submitted by Iraq pursuant to this resolution and failure to comply with, and co-operate fully in the interpretation of, this resolution'."

474. It is unclear what specific grounds Mr Blair relied upon in reaching his view.

475. In his advice of 7 March, Lord Goldsmith had said that the views of UNMOVIC and the IAEA would be highly significant in demonstrating hard evidence of non-compliance and non-co-operation. In the exchange of letters on 14 and 15 March between Mr Brummell and No.10, there is no reference to their views; the only view referred to was that of Mr Blair.

476. Following receipt of Mr Brummell's letter of 14 March, Mr Blair neither requested nor received considered advice addressing the evidence on which he expressed his "unequivocal view" that Iraq was "in further material breach of its obligations".

477. Senior Ministers should have considered the question posed in Mr Brummell's letter of 14 March, either in the Defence and Overseas Policy Committee or a "War Cabinet", on the basis of formal advice. Such a Committee should then have reported its conclusions to Cabinet before its members were asked to endorse the Government's policy.

Lord Goldsmith's Written Answer of 17 March 2003

478. In Parliament during the second week of March, and in the media, there were calls on the Government to make a statement about its legal position.

479. When Lord Goldsmith spoke to Mr Brummell on 13 March, they agreed that a statement should be prepared "setting out the Attorney's view of the legal position which could be deployed at Cabinet and in Parliament the following week".

480. The message was conveyed to No.10 during the morning of 15 March that Lord Goldsmith "would make clear during the course of the week that there is a sound legal basis for action should that prove necessary".

481. The decision that Lord Goldsmith would take the lead in explaining the Government's legal position to Parliament, rather than the Prime Minister or responsible Secretary of State providing that explanation, was unusual.

482. The normal practice was, and is, that the Minister responsible for the policy, in this case Mr Blair or Mr Straw, would have made such a statement.

Cabinet, 17 March 2003

483. Cabinet was provided with the text of Lord Goldsmith's Written Answer to Baroness Ramsey of Cartvale setting out the legal basis for military action.

484. That document represented a statement of the Government's legal position – it did not explain the legal basis of the conclusion that Iraq had failed to take "the final opportunity" to comply with its disarmament obligations offered by resolution 1441.

485. Lord Goldsmith told Cabinet that it was "plain" that Iraq had failed to comply with its obligations and continued to be in "material breach" of the relevant Security Council resolutions. The authority to use force under resolution 678 was, "as a result", revived. Lord Goldsmith said that there was no need for a further resolution.

486. Cabinet was not provided with written advice which set out, as the advice of 7 March had done, the conflicting arguments regarding the legal effect of resolution 1441 and whether, in particular, it authorised military action without a further resolution of the Security Council.

487. Cabinet was not provided with, or informed of, Mr Brummell's letter to Mr Rycroft of 14 March; or Mr Rycroft's response of 15 March. Cabinet was not told how Mr Blair had reached the view recorded in Mr Rycroft's letter.

488. The majority of Cabinet members who gave evidence to the Inquiry took the position that the role of the Attorney General on 17 March was, simply, to tell Cabinet whether or not there was a legal basis for military action.

489. None of those Ministers who had read Lord Goldsmith's 7 March advice asked for an explanation as to why his legal view of resolution 1441 had changed.

490. There was little appetite to question Lord Goldsmith about his advice, and no substantive discussion of the legal issues was recorded.

491. Cabinet was not misled on 17 March and the exchange of letters between the Attorney General's office and No.10 on 14 and 15 March did not constitute, as suggested to the Inquiry by Ms Short, a "side deal".

492. Cabinet was, however, being asked to confirm the decision that the diplomatic process was at an end and that the House of Commons should be asked to endorse the use of military action to enforce Iraq's compliance. Given the gravity of this decision, Cabinet should have been made aware of the legal uncertainties.

493. Lord Goldsmith should have been asked to provide written advice which fully reflected the position on 17 March, explained the legal basis on which the UK could take military action and set out the risks of legal challenge.

494. The advice should have addressed the significance of the exchange of letters of 14 and 15 March and how, in the absence of agreement from the majority of members of the Security Council, the point had been reached that Iraq had failed to take the final opportunity offered by resolution 1441.

495. The advice should have been provided to Ministers and senior officials whose responsibilities were directly engaged and should have been made available to Cabinet.

Weapons of mass destruction

Iraq WMD assessments, pre-July 2002

496. The ingrained belief that Saddam Hussein's regime retained chemical and biological warfare capabilities, was determined to preserve and if possible enhance its capabilities, including at some point in the future a nuclear capability, and was pursuing an active policy of deception and concealment, had underpinned UK policy towards Iraq since the Gulf Conflict ended in 1991.

497. While the detail of individual JIC Assessments on Iraq varied, this core construct remained in place.

498. Security Council resolutions adopted since 1991 demanded Iraq's disarmament and the re-admission of inspectors, and imposed sanctions in the absence of Iraqi compliance with those – and other – obligations. Agreement to those resolutions indicated that doubts about whether Iraq had disarmed were widely shared.

499. In parallel, by 2000, the wider risk of proliferation was regarded as a major threat. There was heightened concern about:

- the danger of proliferation, particularly that countries of concern might obtain nuclear weapons and ballistic missiles; and
- the potential risk that terrorist groups which were willing to use them might gain access to chemical and biological agents and, possibly, nuclear material, and the means to deliver them.

500. These concerns were reinforced after 9/11.

501. The view conveyed in JIC Assessments between December 2000 and March 2002 was that, despite the considerable achievements of UNSCOM and the IAEA between 1991 and December 1998, including dismantling Iraq's nuclear programme, the inspectors had been unable to account for some of the ballistic missiles and chemical and biological weapons and material produced by Iraq; and that it had:

- not totally destroyed all its stockpile of chemical and biological weapons;
- retained up to 360 tonnes of chemical agents and precursor chemicals and growth media which would allow it to produce more chemical and biological agents;
- hidden a small number of long-range Al Hussein ballistic missiles; and
- retained the knowledge, documentation and personnel which would allow it to reconstitute its chemical, biological, nuclear and ballistic missile programmes.

502. The JIC also judged that, since the departure of the weapons inspectors, Iraq:

- was actively pursuing programmes to extend the range of its existing short-range ballistic missiles beyond the permitted range of 150km;
- had begun development of a ballistic missile with a range greater than 1,000km;
- was capable of resuming undetected production of "significant quantities" of chemical and biological agents, and in the case of VX (a nerve agent) might have already done so; and
- was pursuing activities that could be linked to a nuclear programme.

503. Iraq's chemical, biological and ballistic missile programmes were seen as a threat to international peace and security in the Middle East region, but Iraq was viewed as a less serious proliferation threat than other key countries of concern – Iran, Libya and North Korea – which had current nuclear programmes. Iraq's nuclear facilities had been dismantled by the weapons inspectors. The JIC judged that Iraq would be unable to obtain a nuclear weapon while sanctions remained effective.

504. The JIC continued to judge that co-operation between Iraq and Al Qaida was "unlikely", and that there was no "credible evidence of Iraqi transfers of WMD-related technology and expertise to terrorist groups".

505. In mid-February 2002, in preparation for Mr Blair's planned meeting with President Bush in early April 2002, No.10 commissioned the preparation of a paper to inform the public about the dangers of nuclear proliferation and WMD more generally in four key countries of concern, North Korea, Iran, Libya and Iraq.

506. When the preparation of this document became public knowledge, it was perceived to be intended to underpin a decision on military action against Iraq. The content and timing became a sensitive issue.

507. Reflecting the UK position that action was needed to disarm Iraq, Mr Blair and Mr Straw began, from late February 2002, publicly to argue that Iraq was a threat which had to be dealt with; that Iraq needed to disarm or be disarmed in accordance with the

obligations imposed by the UN; and that it was important to agree to the return of UN inspectors to Iraq.

508. The focus on Iraq was not the result of a step change in Iraq's capabilities or intentions.

509. When he saw the draft paper on WMD countries of concern on 8 March, Mr Straw commented:

> "Good, but should not Iraq be <u>first</u> and also have more text? The paper has to show why there is an <u>exceptional</u> threat from Iraq. It does not quite do this yet."[200]

510. On 18 March, Mr Straw decided that a paper on Iraq should be issued before one addressing other countries of concern.

511. On 22 March, Mr Straw was advised that the evidence would not convince public opinion that there was an imminent threat from Iraq. Publication was postponed.

512. No.10 decided that the Cabinet Office Overseas and Defence Secretariat should co-ordinate the production of a "public dossier" on Iraq, and that Mr Campbell should "retain the lead role on the timing/form of its release".

513. The statements prepared for, and used by, the UK Government in public, from late 2001 onwards, about Iraq's proscribed activities and the potential threat they posed were understandably written in more direct and less nuanced language than the JIC Assessments on which they drew.

514. The question is whether, in doing so, they conveyed more certainty and knowledge than was justified, or created tests it would be impossible for Iraq to meet. That is of particular concern in relation to the evidence in Section 4.1 on two key issues.

515. First, the estimates of the weapons and material related to Iraq's chemical and biological warfare programmes for which UNSCOM had been unable to account were based on extrapolations from UNSCOM records. Officials explicitly advised that it was "inherently difficult to arrive at precise figures". In addition, it was acknowledged that neither UNSCOM nor the UK could be certain about either exactly what had existed or what Iraq had already destroyed.

516. The revised estimates announced by Mr Straw on 2 May were increasingly presented in Government statements as the benchmark against which Iraq should be judged.

517. Second, the expert MOD examination of issues in late March 2002 exposed the difficulties Iraq would have to overcome before it could acquire a nuclear weapon. That included the difficulty of acquiring suitable fissile material from the "black market".

---

[200] Minute McDonald to Ricketts, 11 March 2002, 'Iraq'.

518. In addition, the tendency to refer in public statements only to Iraq's "weapons of mass destruction" without addressing their nature (the type of warhead and whether they were battlefield or strategic weapons systems) or how they might be used (as a last resort against invading military forces or as a weapon of terror to threaten civilian populations in other countries) was likely to have created the impression that Iraq posed a greater threat than the detailed JIC Assessments would have supported.

Iraq WMD assessments, July to September 2002

519. From late February 2002, the UK Government position was that Iraq was a threat that had to be dealt with; that Iraq needed to disarm in accordance with the obligations imposed by the UN; and that it was important to agree to the return of UN inspectors to Iraq.

520. The urgency and certainty with which the position was stated reflected both the ingrained beliefs already described and the wider context in which the policy was being discussed with the US.

521. But it also served to fuel the demand that the Government should publish the document it was known to have prepared, setting out the reasons why it was so concerned about Iraq.

522. In the spring and summer of 2002, senior officials and Ministers took the view that the Iraq dossier should not be published until the way ahead on the policy was clearer.

523. By late August 2002, the Government was troubled by intense speculation about whether a decision had already been taken to use military force. In Mr Blair's words, the US and UK had been "outed" as having taken a decision when no such decision had been taken.

524. Mr Blair's decision on 3 September to announce that the dossier would be published was a response to that pressure.

525. The dossier was designed to "make the case" and secure Parliamentary (and public) support for the Government's position that action was urgently required to secure Iraq's disarmament.

526. The UK Government intended the information and judgements in the Iraq dossier to be seen to be the product of the JIC in order to carry authority with Parliament and the public.

527. The Secret Intelligence Service (SIS) was commissioned by No.10 on 5 September to examine whether it had any additional material which could be included.

528. Mr Scarlett, as Chairman of the JIC, was given the responsibility of producing the dossier.

529. The dossier drew on the 9 September JIC Assessment, 'Iraqi Use of Chemical and Biological Weapons – Possible Scenarios', which had been commissioned to address scenarios for Iraq's possible use of chemical and biological weapons in the event of military action, previous JIC Assessments and the subsequent report issued by SIS on 11 September.

530. The SIS report should have been shown to the relevant experts in the Defence Intelligence Staff (DIS) who could have advised their senior managers and the Assessments Staff.

531. Expert officials in DIS questioned the certainty with which some of the judgements in the dossier were expressed. Some of their questions were discussed during the preparation of the dossier. The text was agreed by Air Marshal Joe French, Chief of Defence Intelligence, at the JIC meeting on 19 September.

532. There is no evidence that other members of the JIC were aware at the time of the reservations recorded in the minute by Dr Brian Jones (the branch head of the nuclear, biological and chemical section in the Scientific and Technical Directorate of the Defence Intelligence Staff) of 19 September and that written by the chemical weapons expert in his team the following day.

533. The JIC accepted ownership of the dossier and agreed its content. There is no evidence that intelligence was improperly included in the dossier or that No.10 improperly influenced the text.

534. At issue are the judgements made by the JIC and how they and the intelligence were presented, including in Mr Blair's Foreword and in his statement to Parliament on 24 September 2002.

535. It is unlikely that Parliament and the public would have distinguished between the ownership and therefore the authority of the judgements in the Foreword and those in the Executive Summary and the main body of the dossier.

536. In the Foreword, Mr Blair stated that he believed the "assessed intelligence" had "established beyond doubt" that Saddam Hussein had "continued to produce chemical and biological weapons, that he continues in his efforts to develop nuclear weapons, and that he had been able to extend the range of his ballistic missile programme". That raises two key questions.

- Did Mr Blair's statements in whole or in part go further than the assessed intelligence?
- Did that matter?

537. The Inquiry is not questioning Mr Blair's belief, which he consistently reiterated in his evidence to the Inquiry, or his legitimate role in advocating Government policy.

538. But the deliberate selection of a formulation which grounded the statement in what Mr Blair believed, rather than in the judgements which the JIC had actually reached in its assessment of the intelligence, indicates a distinction between his beliefs and the JIC's actual judgements.

539. That is supported by the position taken by the JIC and No.10 officials at the time, and in the evidence offered to the Inquiry by some of those involved.

540. The assessed intelligence had <u>not</u> established beyond doubt that Saddam Hussein had continued to produce chemical and biological weapons. The Executive Summary of the dossier stated that the JIC judged that Iraq had "continued to produce chemical and biological agents". The main text of the dossier said that there had been "recent" production. It also stated that Iraq had the means to deliver chemical and biological weapons. It did not say that Iraq had continued to produce weapons.

541. Nor had the assessed intelligence established beyond doubt that efforts to develop nuclear weapons continued. The JIC stated in the Executive Summary of the dossier that Iraq had:

- made covert attempts "to acquire technology and materials which could be used in the production of nuclear weapons";
- "sought significant quantities of uranium from Africa, despite having no active nuclear programme that would require it"; and
- "recalled specialists to work on its nuclear programme".

542. But the dossier made clear that, as long as sanctions remained effective, Iraq could not produce a nuclear weapon.

543. These conclusions draw on the evidence from the JIC Assessments at the time and the Executive Summary of the dossier, which are set out in Section 4.2. They do not rely on hindsight.

544. The JIC itself should have made that position clear because its ownership of the dossier, which was intended to inform a highly controversial policy debate, carried with it the responsibility to ensure that the JIC's integrity was protected.

545. The process of seeking the JIC's views, through Mr Scarlett, on the text of the Foreword shows that No.10 expected the JIC to raise any concerns it had.

546. The firmness of Mr Blair's beliefs, despite the underlying uncertainties, is important in considering how the judgements in the Foreword would have been interpreted by Cabinet in its discussions on 23 September and by Parliament.

547. In his statement to Parliament on 24 September and in his answers to subsequent questions, Mr Blair presented Iraq's past, current and potential future capabilities as evidence of the severity of the potential threat from Iraq's weapons of mass destruction; and that, at some point in the future, that threat would become a reality.

548. By the time the dossier was published, President Bush had announced that the US was seeking action on Iraq through the UN, and Iraq had agreed to the return of inspectors.

549. Rather than the debate being framed in terms of the answers needed to the outstanding questions identified by UNSCOM and the IAEA, including the material for which UNSCOM had been unable to account, the dossier's description of Iraq's capabilities and intent became part of the baseline against which the UK Government measured Iraq's future statements and actions and the success of weapons inspections.

550. As Section 4.3 demonstrates, the judgements remained in place without challenge until the invasion of Iraq in March 2003. Iraq's denials of the capabilities and intent attributed to it were not taken seriously.

551. As the flaws in the construct and the intelligence were exposed after the conflict, the dossier and subsequent statements to Parliament also became the baseline against which the Government's good faith and credibility were judged.

Iraq WMD assessments, October 2002 to March 2003

552. From October 2002 onwards, the JIC focused on two main themes:

- Iraq's attitude to the return of the inspectors and, from 8 November, its compliance with the specific obligations imposed by resolution 1441; and

- Iraq's options, diplomatic and military, including the possible use of chemical and biological weapons and ballistic missiles against Coalition Forces or countries in the region in either pre-emptive attacks or in response to a military attack.

553. In its Assessment of 18 December, the JIC made the judgements in the UK Government September dossier part of the test for Iraq.

554. The judgements about Iraq's capabilities and intentions relied heavily on Iraq's past behaviour being a reliable indicator of its current and future actions.

555. There was no consideration of whether, faced with the prospect of a US-led invasion, Saddam Hussein had taken a different position.

556. The absence of evidence of proscribed programmes and materials relating to the production or delivery of chemical, biological or nuclear weapons was attributed to Iraq's ability to conceal its activities and deceive the inspectors and the difficulties which it had been anticipated the inspectors would encounter.

557. The JIC Assessment of 11 October 2002 stated that a good intelligence flow from inside Iraq, supporting tougher inspections, would be "central to success".

558. A key element of the Assessments was the reporting and intelligence on Iraq's intentions to conceal its activities, deceive the inspectors and obstruct the conduct of inspections, particularly Iraq's attitudes to preventing interviews with officials who were identified as associated with its proscribed programmes or who had been involved in Iraq's unilateral destruction of its weapons and facilities.

559. The large number of intelligence reports about Iraq's activities were interpreted from the perspective that Iraq's objectives were to conceal its programmes.

560. Similarly, Iraq's actions were consistently interpreted as indicative of deceit.

561. From early 2003, the Government drew heavily on the intelligence reporting of Iraq's activities to deceive and obstruct the inspectors to illustrate its conclusion that Iraq had no intention of complying with the obligations imposed in resolution 1441.

562. The Government also emphasised the reliability of the reporting.

563. The JIC's judgement from August 2002 until 19 March 2003 remained that Iraq might use chemical and biological weapons in response to a military attack.

564. Iraq's statements that it had no weapons or programmes were dismissed as further evidence of a strategy of denial.

565. In addition, the extent to which the JIC's judgements depended on inference and interpretation of Iraq's previous attitudes and behaviour was not recognised.

566. At no stage was the hypothesis that Iraq might not have chemical, biological or nuclear weapons or programmes identified and examined by either the JIC or the policy community.

567. After its 9 September 2002 Assessment, the JIC was not asked to review its judgements on Iraq's capabilities and programmes which underpinned UK thinking. Nor did the JIC itself suggest such a review.

568. As a result there was no formal reassessment of the JIC judgements, and the 9 September Assessment and the 24 September dossier provided part of the baseline for the UK Government's view of Iraq's capabilities and intentions on its chemical, biological, nuclear and ballistic missile programmes.

569. Given the weight which rested on the JIC's judgements about Iraq's possession of WMD and its future intent for the decision in March that military action should, if necessary, be taken to disarm Iraq, a formal reassessment of the JIC's judgements should have taken place.

570. This might have been prompted by Dr Blix's report to the Security Council on 14 February 2003, which demonstrated the developing divergence between the assessments presented by the US and UK. Dr Blix's report of 7 March, which changed the view that Iraqi behaviour was preventing UNMOVIC from carrying out its tasks, should certainly have prompted a review.

The search for WMD

571. Section 4.4 considers the impact of the failure to find stockpiles of WMD in Iraq in the months immediately after the invasion, and of the emerging conclusions of the Iraq Survey Group (ISG), on:

- the Government's response to demands for an independent judge-led inquiry into pre-conflict intelligence on Iraq; and
- the Government's public presentation of the nature of the threat from Saddam Hussein's regime and the decision to go to war.

572. The Inquiry has not sought to comment in detail on the specific conclusions of the ISC, FAC, Hutton and Butler Reports, all of which were published before the withdrawal by SIS in September 2004 of a significant proportion of the intelligence underpinning the JIC Assessments and September 2002 dossier on which UK policy had rested.

573. In addition to the conclusions of those reports, the Inquiry notes the forthright statement in March 2005 of the US Commission on the Intelligence Capabilities of the United States Regarding Weapons of Mass Destruction. Reporting to President Bush, the Commission stated that "the [US] Intelligence Community was dead wrong in almost all of its pre-war judgments about Iraq's weapons of mass destruction. This was a major intelligence failure."

574. The evidence in Section 4.4 shows that, after the invasion, the UK Government, including the intelligence community, was reluctant to admit, and to recognise publicly, the mounting evidence that there had been failings in the UK's pre-conflict collection, validation, analysis and presentation of intelligence on Iraq's WMD.

575. Despite the failure to identify any evidence of WMD programmes during pre-conflict inspections, the UK Government remained confident that evidence would be found after the Iraqi regime had been removed.

576. Almost immediately after the start of the invasion, UK Ministers and officials sought to lower public expectations of immediate or significant finds of WMD in Iraq.

577. The lack of evidence to support pre-conflict claims about Iraq's WMD challenged the credibility of the Government and the intelligence community, and the legitimacy of the war.

578. The Government and the intelligence community were both concerned about the consequences of the presentational aspects of their pre-war assessments being discredited.

579. By June, the Government had acknowledged the need for a review of the UK's pre-conflict intelligence on Iraq. It responded to demands for an independent, judge-led inquiry by expressing support for the reviews initiated by the ISC and the FAC.

580. The announcement of the Hutton Inquiry into the circumstances surrounding the death of Dr David Kelly on 18 July, reinforced the Government's position that additional reviews were not needed.

581. The Government maintained that position until January 2004, backed by three votes in the House of Commons (on 4 June, 15 July and 22 October 2003) rejecting a succession of Opposition motions calling for an independent inquiry into the use of pre-war intelligence.

582. Mr Blair's initial response to growing criticism of the failure to find WMD was to counsel patience.

583. After the publication of the ISG Interim Report, the Government's focus shifted from finding stockpiles of weapons to emphasising evidence of the Iraqi regime's strategic intent.

584. Once President Bush made clear his decision to set up an independent inquiry, Mr Blair's resistance to a public inquiry became untenable.

585. After the announcement of the Butler Review, the UK Government's focus shifted to the content of the next ISG report, the Status Report.

586. The Government, still concerned about the nature of the public debate on WMD in the UK, sought to ensure that the Status Report included existing ISG material highlighting the strategic intentions of Saddam Hussein's regime and breaches of Security Council resolutions.

587. Mr Blair remained concerned about continuing public and Parliamentary criticism of the pre-conflict intelligence, the failure to find WMD and the decision to invade Iraq. After the reports from the Hutton Inquiry, the ISG and the US Commission, he sought to demonstrate that, although "the exact basis for action was not as we thought", the invasion had still been justified.

588. The ISG's findings were significant, but did not support past statements by the UK and US Governments, which had focused on Iraq's current capabilities and an urgent and growing threat.

589. The explanation for military action put forward by Mr Blair in October 2004 was not the one given before the conflict.

Planning for a post-Saddam Hussein Iraq

The failure to plan or prepare for known risks

590. The information on Iraq available to the UK Government before the invasion provided a clear indication of the potential scale of the post-conflict task.

591. It showed that, in order to achieve the UK's desired end state, any post-conflict administration would need to:

- restore infrastructure that had deteriorated significantly in the decade since 1991, to the point where it was not capable of meeting the needs of the Iraqi people;

- administer a state where the upper echelons of a regime that had been in power since 1968 had been abruptly removed and in which the capabilities of the wider civil administration, many of whose employees were members of the ruling party, were difficult to assess; and

- provide security in a country faced with a number of potential threats, including:
  - internecine violence;
  - terrorism; and
  - Iranian interference.

592. In December 2002, the MOD described the post-conflict phase of operations as "strategically decisive".[201] But when the invasion began, the UK Government was not in a position to conclude that satisfactory plans had been drawn up and preparations made to meet known post-conflict challenges and risks in Iraq and to mitigate the risk of strategic failure.

593. Throughout the planning process, the UK assumed that the US would be responsible for preparing the post-conflict plan, that post-conflict activity would be authorised by the UN Security Council, that agreement would be reached on a significant post-conflict role for the UN and that international partners would step forward to share the post-conflict burden.

594. On that basis, the UK planned to reduce its military contribution in Iraq to medium scale within four months of the start of the invasion[202] and expected not to have to make a substantial commitment to post-conflict administration.[203]

595. Achieving that outcome depended on the UK's ability to persuade the US of the merits of a significant post-conflict role for the UN.

596. The UK could not be certain at any stage in the year before the invasion that it would succeed in that aim.

597. In January 2003, the UK sought to persuade the US of the benefits of UN leadership of Iraq's interim post-conflict civil administration.[204] Officials warned that,

---

[201] Paper [SPG], 13 December 2002, 'UK Military Strategic Thinking on Iraq'.

[202] Minute CDS to CJO, 18 March 2003, 'Op TELIC: Authorisation for Military Operations in Iraq' attaching Paper CDS, 'Chief of Defence Staff Execute Directive to the Joint Commander for Operation TELIC (Phases 3 and 4)'.

[203] Minute Straw and Hoon to Prime Minister, 19 March 2003, 'Iraq: UK Military Contribution to post-conflict Iraq'.

[204] Minute Ricketts to Private Secretary [FCO], 7 February 2003, 'Iraq Strategy'.

if the UK failed to persuade the US, it risked "being drawn into a huge commitment of UK resources for a highly complex task of administration and law and order for an uncertain period".

598. By March 2003, having failed to persuade the US of the advantages of a UN-led interim administration, the UK had set the less ambitious goal of persuading the US to accept UN authorisation of a Coalition-led interim administration and an international presence that would include the UN.[205]

599. On 19 March, Mr Blair stated in Parliament that discussions were taking place with the US, UN and others on the role of the UN and post-conflict issues.[206]

600. Discussions continued, but, as the invasion began:

- The UK had not secured US agreement to a Security Council resolution authorising post-conflict administration and could not be sure when, or on what terms, agreement would be possible.

- The extent of the UN's preparations, which had been hindered by the absence of agreement on post-conflict arrangements, remained uncertain. Mr Annan emphasised to Ms Short the need for clarity on US thinking so that UN planning could proceed[207] and told Sir Jeremy Greenstock that he "would not wish to see any arrangement subjugating UN activity to Coalition activity".[208]

- Potential international partners for reconstruction and additional Coalition partners to provide security continued to make their post-conflict contributions conditional on UN authorisation for Phase IV (the military term for post-conflict operations).[209]

601. Despite being aware of the shortcomings of the US plan,[210] strong US resistance to a leading role for the UN,[211] indications that the UN did not want the administration of Iraq to become its responsibility[212] and a warning about the tainted image of the UN in Iraq,[213] at no stage did the UK Government formally consider other policy options, including the possibility of making participation in military action conditional on a satisfactory plan for the post-conflict period, or how to mitigate the known risk that the UK could find itself drawn into a "huge commitment of UK resources" for which no contingency preparations had been made.

---

[205] Paper Iraq Planning Unit, 25 March 2003, 'Iraq: Phase IV: Authorising UNSCR'.
[206] House of Commons, *Official Report*, 19 March 2003, columns 931-932.
[207] Telegram 501 UKMIS New York to FCO London, 21 March 2003, 'Iraq Humanitarian/Reconstruction: Clare Short's Visit to New York'.
[208] Telegram 526 UKMIS New York to FCO London, 25 March 2003, 'Iraq Phase IV: UN Dynamics'.
[209] Paper FCO, 25 March 2003, 'Iraq: Phase IV Issues'.
[210] Minute Drummond to Rycroft, 19 March 2003, 'Iraq Ministerial Meeting'.
[211] Minute Ricketts to Private Secretary [FCO], 7 February 2003, 'Iraq Strategy'.
[212] Public hearing, 15 December 2009, page 5.
[213] Paper Middle East Department, 12 December 2002, 'Interim Administrations in Iraq: Why a UN-led Interim Administration would be in the US interest'.

The planning process and decision-making

602. As a junior partner in the Coalition, the UK worked within a planning framework established by the US. It had limited influence over a process dominated increasingly by the US military.

603. The creation of the Ad Hoc Group on Iraq in September 2002 and the Iraq Planning Unit in February 2003 improved co-ordination across government at official level, but neither body carried sufficient authority to establish a unified planning process across the four principal departments involved – the FCO, the MOD, DFID and the Treasury – or between military and civilian planners.

604. Important material, including in the DFID reviews of northern and southern Iraq, and significant pieces of analysis, including the series of MOD Strategic Planning Group (SPG) papers on military strategic thinking, were either not shared outside the originating department, or, as appears to have been the case with the SPG papers, were not routinely available to all those with a direct interest in the contents.

605. Some risks were identified, but departmental ownership of those risks, and responsibility for analysis and mitigation, were not clearly established.

606. When the need to plan and prepare for the worst case was raised, including by MOD officials in advice to Mr Hoon on 6 March 2003,[214] Lieutenant General John Reith, Chief of Joint Operations, in his paper for the Chiefs of Staff on 21 March[215] and in Treasury advice to Mr Brown on 24 March,[216] there is no evidence that any department or individual assumed ownership or was assigned responsibility for analysis or mitigation. No action ensued.

607. In April 2003, Mr Blair set up the Ad Hoc Ministerial Group on Iraq Rehabilitation (AHMGIR), chaired by Mr Straw, to oversee the UK contribution to post-conflict reconstruction.

608. Until the creation of the AHMGIR, Mr Straw, Mr Hoon and Ms Short remained jointly responsible for directing post-conflict planning and preparation.

609. In the absence of a single person responsible for overseeing all aspects of planning and preparation, departments pursued complementary, but separate, objectives. Gaps in UK capabilities were overlooked.

610. The FCO, which focused on policy-making and negotiation, was not equipped by past experience or practice, or by its limited human and financial resources, to prepare for nation-building of the scale required in Iraq, and did not expect to do so.

------

[214] Minute Sec(O)4 to PS/Secretary of State [MOD], 6 March 2003, 'Iraq: Aftermath – Medium to Long Term UK Military Commitment'.
[215] Minute Reith to COSSEC, 21 March 2003, 'Phase IV Planning – Taking Stock'.
[216] Minute Dodds to Chancellor, 24 March 2003, 'Iraq: UK Military Contribution to Post-Conflict Iraq'.

611. DFID's focus on poverty reduction and the channelling of assistance through multilateral institutions instilled a reluctance, before the invasion, to engage on anything other than the immediate humanitarian response to conflict.

612. When military planners advised of the need to consider the civilian component as an integral part of the UK's post-conflict deployment, the Government was not equipped to respond. Neither the FCO nor DFID took responsibility for the issue.

613. The shortage of expertise in reconstruction and stabilisation was a constraint on the planning process and on the contribution the UK was able to make to the administration and reconstruction of post-conflict Iraq.

614. The UK Government's post-invasion response to the shortage of deployable experts in stabilisation and post-conflict reconstruction is addressed in Section 10.3.

615. Constraints on UK military capacity are addressed in Sections 6.1 and 6.2.

616. The UK contribution to the post-conflict humanitarian response is assessed in Section 10.1.

617. At no stage did Ministers or senior officials commission the systematic evaluation of different options, incorporating detailed analysis of risk and UK capabilities, military and civilian, which should have been required before the UK committed to any course of action in Iraq.

618. Where policy recommendations were supported by untested assumptions, those assumptions were seldom challenged. When they were, the issue was not always followed through.

619. It was the responsibility of officials to identify, analyse and advise on risk and Ministers' responsibility to ensure that measures to mitigate identifiable risks, including a range of policy options, had been considered before significant decisions were taken on the direction of UK policy.

620. Occasions when that would have been appropriate included:

- after Mr Blair's meeting with Mr Hoon, Mr Straw and others on 23 July 2002;
- after the adoption of resolution 1441;
- before or immediately after the decision to deploy troops in January 2003;
- after the Rock Drill (a US inter-agency rehearsal for post-conflict administration) in February 2003; and
- after Mr Blair's meeting on post-conflict issues on 6 March 2003.

621. There is no indication of formal risk analysis or formal consideration of options associated with any of those events.

622. In his statement to the Inquiry, Mr Blair said:

"... with hindsight, we now see that the military campaign to defeat Saddam was relatively easy; it was the aftermath that was hard. At the time, of course, we could not know that and a prime focus throughout was the military campaign itself ..."[217]

623. The conclusions reached by Mr Blair after the invasion did not require the benefit of hindsight.

624. Mr Blair's long-standing conviction that successful international intervention required long-term commitment had been clearly expressed in his Chicago speech in 1999.

625. That conviction was echoed, in the context of Iraq, in frequent advice to Mr Blair from Ministers and officials.

626. Between early 2002 and the invasion of Iraq in March 2003, Mr Blair received warnings about:

- the significance of the post-conflict phase as the "strategically decisive" phase of the engagement in Iraq (in the SPG paper of 13 December 2002[218]) and the risk that a badly handled aftermath would make intervention a "net failure" (in the letter from Mr Hoon's Private Office to Sir David Manning of 19 November 2002[219]);

- the likelihood of internal conflict in Iraq (including from Mr Powell on 26 September 2002, who warned of the need to stop "a terrible bloodletting of revenge after Saddam goes. Traditional in Iraq after conflict"[220]);

- the potential scale of the political, social, economic and security challenge (including from Sir Christopher Meyer (British Ambassador to the US) on 6 September 2002: "it will probably make pacifying Afghanistan look like child's play"[221]);

- the need for an analysis of whether the benefits of military action outweighed the risk of a protracted and costly nation-building exercise (including from Mr Straw on 8 July 2002: the US "must also understand that we are serious about our conditions for UK involvement"[222]);

- the absence of credible US plans for the immediate post-conflict period and the subsequent reconstruction of Iraq (including from the British Embassy

---

[217] Statement Blair, 14 January 2011, page 14.
[218] Paper [SPG], 13 December 2002, 'UK Military Strategic Thinking on Iraq'.
[219] Letter Watkins to Manning, 19 November 2002, 'Iraq: Military Planning after UNSCR 1441'.
[220] Manuscript comment Powell to Manning on Letter McDonald to Manning, 26 September 2002, 'Scenarios for the future of Iraq after Saddam'.
[221] Telegram 1140 Washington to FCO London, 6 September 2002, 'PM's visit to Camp David: Iraq'.
[222] Letter Straw to Prime Minister, 8 July 2002, 'Iraq: Contingency Planning'.

Washington after the Rock Drill on 21 and 22 February 2003: "The inter-agency rehearsal for Phase IV … exposes the enormous scale of the task … Overall, planning is at a very rudimentary stage"[223]);

- the need to agree with the US the nature of the UK contribution to those plans (including in the letter from Mr Hoon's Private Office to Sir David Manning on 28 February 2003: it was "absolutely clear" that the US expected the UK to take leadership of the South-East sector. The UK was "currently at risk of taking on a very substantial commitment that we will have great difficulty in sustaining beyond the immediate conclusion of conflict"[224]); and

- the importance (including in the 'UK overall plan for Phase IV', shown to Mr Blair on 7 March 2003[225]) of:

  o UN authorisation for the military occupation of Iraq, without which there would be no legal cover for certain post-conflict tasks;

  o a UN framework for the administration and reconstruction of Iraq during the transition to Iraqi self-government.

627. Mr Blair told the Chiefs of Staff on 15 January 2003 that "the 'Issue' was aftermath – the Coalition must prevent anarchy and internecine fighting breaking out".[226]

628. In his evidence to the House of Commons Liaison Committee on 21 January 2003, Mr Blair emphasised the importance of the post-conflict phase:

"You do not engage in military conflict that may produce regime change unless you are prepared to follow through and work in the aftermath of that regime change to ensure the country is stable and the people are properly looked after."[227]

629. On 24 January 2003, Mr Blair told President Bush that the biggest risk they faced was internecine fighting, and that delay would allow time for working up more coherent post-conflict plans.[228]

630. Yet when Mr Blair set out the UK's vision for the future of Iraq in the House of Commons on 18 March 2003, no assessment had been made of whether that vision was achievable, no agreement had been reached with the US on a workable post-conflict plan, UN authorisation had not yet been secured, and there had been no decision on the UN's role in post-conflict Iraq.

---

[223] Telegram 235 Washington to FCO London, 24 February 2003, 'Iraq: Day After: Rehearsal of Office of Reconstruction and Humanitarian Assistance'.
[224] Letter Williams to Manning, 28 February 2003, 'Iraq: Military Planning and Preparation' attaching Paper [unattributed], 28 February 2003, 'Iraq: Military Planning Update – 28 February 2003'.
[225] Paper Iraq Planning Unit, 7 March 2003, 'The UK overall plan for Phase IV'.
[226] Minute MA/DCJO to MA/CJO, 15 January 2003, 'Briefing to Prime Minister'.
[227] Liaison Committee, Session 2002-2003, Minutes of Evidence Taken Before the Liaison Committee Tuesday 21 January 2003, Q 117.
[228] Letter Manning to Rice, 24 January 2003, [untitled] attaching 'Note'.

631. UK policy rested on the assumption that:

- the US would provide effective leadership of the immediate post-conflict effort in Iraq;
- the conditions would soon be in place for UK military withdrawal;
- after a short period of US-led, UN-authorised military occupation, the UN would administer and provide a framework for the reconstruction of post-conflict Iraq;
- substantial international support would follow UN authorisation; and
- reconstruction and the political transition to Iraqi rule would proceed in a secure environment.

632. Mr Blair was already aware that those assumptions concealed significant risks:

- UK officials assessed that the Office of Reconstruction and Humanitarian Assistance (ORHA), the US body that would assume responsibility for the immediate post-invasion administration of Iraq, was not up to the task.
- Significant differences remained between UK and US positions on UN involvement, and between the UK and the UN.
- International partners were scarce and thought to be unlikely to come forward in the absence of UN authorisation.
- UK officials recognised that occupying forces would not remain welcome for long and threats to security could quickly escalate.

633. In the year before the invasion, Mr Blair:

- stated his belief in the importance of post-conflict planning on several occasions, including in Cabinet, in Parliament and with President Bush;
- requested advice on aspects of post-conflict Iraq (including for his summer reading pack in July 2002, for his meeting with President Bush on 31 January 2003, and twice in February 2003 after reading the JIC Assessment of southern Iraq and the Adelphi Paper *Iraq at the Crossroads*);
- at the meeting with Mr Hoon and the Chiefs of Staff on 15 January 2003, asked the MOD to consider the "big 'what ifs'" in the specific context of the UK military plan;
- convened a Ministerial meeting on post-conflict issues on 6 March 2003;
- raised concerns about the state of planning with President Bush; and
- succeeded in the narrow goal of securing President Bush's agreement that the UN should be "heavily involved" in "the post-conflict situation", a loose formulation that appeared to bridge the gap between US and UK positions on UN authorisation and the post-conflict role of the UN, but did not address the substantive issues.

634. Mr Blair did not:

- establish clear Ministerial oversight of post-conflict strategy, planning and preparation;

- ensure that Ministers took the decisions needed to prepare a flexible, realistic and fully resourced plan integrating UK military and civilian contributions;

- seek adequate assurances that the UK was in a position to meet its likely obligations in Iraq;

- insist that the UK's strategic objectives for Iraq were tested against anything other than the best case: a well-planned and executed US-led and UN-authorised post-conflict operation in a relatively benign security environment;

- press President Bush for definitive assurances about US post-conflict plans or set out clearly to him the strategic risk in underestimating the post-conflict challenge and failing adequately to prepare for the task; or

- consider, or seek advice on, whether the absence of a satisfactory plan was a sufficient threat to UK strategic objectives to require a reassessment of the terms of the UK engagement in Iraq. Despite concerns about the state of US planning, he did not make agreement on a satisfactory post-conflict plan a condition of UK participation in military action.

635. In the weeks immediately following the invasion, Mr Blair's omissions made it more difficult for the UK Government to take an informed decision on the establishment of the UK's post-conflict Area of Responsibility (AOR) in southern Iraq (addressed in more detail in Section 8).

636. In the short to medium term, his omissions increased the risk that the UK would be unable to respond to the unexpected in Iraq.

637. In the longer term, they reduced the likelihood of achieving the UK's strategic objectives in Iraq.

The post-conflict period

Occupation

LOOTING IN BASRA

638. As described in Section 8, UK forces entered Basra City on the night of 6/7 April 2003 and rapidly gained control, meeting less resistance than anticipated. Once the city was under its control, the UK was responsible, as the Occupying Power, for maintenance of law and order. Within its predominantly Shia Area of Operations, the UK assumed that risks to Coalition Forces would be lower than in the so-called "Sunni triangle" controlled by the US.

639. Before the invasion, the JIC and the DIS had each identified that there was a risk of lawlessness breaking out in Iraq, and that it would be important to deal with it swiftly. Others, including Mr Blair, Sir Kevin Tebbit and the Iraq Policy Unit, had recognised the seriousness of that risk.

640. However, the formal authorisation for action in Iraq issued by Adm Boyce on 18 March contained no instruction on how to establish a safe and secure environment if lawlessness broke out as anticipated. Although it was known that Phase IV would begin quickly, no Rules of Engagement for that phase, including for dealing with lawlessness, were created and promulgated before UK troops entered the country.

641. Both before and during the invasion Lt Gen Reith made the absence of instructions to UK forces covering what to do if faced with lawless behaviour by the Iraqi population in Basra explicit to the Chiefs of Staff.

642. Faced with widespread looting after the invasion, and without instructions, UK commanders had to make their own judgements about what to do. Brigadier Graham Binns, commanding the 7 Armoured Brigade which had taken Basra City, told the Inquiry that he had concluded that "the best way to stop looting was just to get to a point where there was nothing left to loot".[229]

643. Although the implementation of tactical plans to deal with lawlessness was properly the responsibility of in-theatre commanders, it was the responsibility of the Chief of the Defence Staff and the Chief of Joint Operations to ensure that appropriate Rules of Engagement were set, and preparations made, to equip commanders on the ground to deal with it effectively. They should have ensured that those steps were taken.

644. The impact of looting was felt primarily by the Iraqi population rather than by Coalition Forces. The latter initially experienced a "honeymoon period",[230] although the situation was far from stabilised.

645. Lt Gen Reith anticipated that UK forces could be reduced to a medium scale effort by the autumn, when he expected the campaign to have reached "some form of 'steady-state'".[231]

646. The JIC correctly judged on 16 April that the local population had high hopes that the Coalition would rapidly improve their lives and that "resentment of the Coalition ... could grow quickly if it is seen to be ineffective, either politically or militarily. Such resentment could lead to violence."[232]

---

[229] Private hearing, 2 June 2010, page 11.
[230] Public hearing Walker, 1 February 2010, page 16.
[231] Minute Reith to SECCOS, 14 April 2003, 'Phase 4: Roulement/Recovery of UK Forces' attaching Paper CJO, 14 April 2003, 'Phase 4 - Roulement/Recovery of UK Land Forces'.
[232] JIC Assessment, 16 April 2003, 'Iraq: The Initial Landscape Post-Saddam'.

647. By the end of April, Mr Hoon had announced that UK troop levels would fall to between 25,000 and 30,000 by the middle of May, from an initial peak of around 46,000.

648. Consequently, by the start of May there was a clearly articulated expectation of a rapid drawdown of UK forces by the autumn despite the identified risk that the consent of the local population was built on potentially vulnerable foundations, which could be undermined rapidly and with serious consequences.

LOOTING IN BAGHDAD

649. In the absence of a functioning Iraqi police force and criminal justice system, and without a clear Coalition Phase IV plan, looting and score-settling became a serious problem in Baghdad soon after the regime fell. The looting of ministry buildings and damage to state-owned infrastructure in particular added to the challenges of the Occupation.

650. Reflecting in June 2004, Mr David Richmond, the Prime Minister's Special Representative on Iraq from March to June 2004, judged that the failure to crack down on looting in Baghdad in April 2003 released "a crime wave which the Coalition has never been able to bring fully under control".[233]

651. After visiting Iraq in early May 2003, General Sir Mike Jackson, Chief of the General Staff, observed:

> "A security vacuum still exists [in Baghdad] ... particularly at night. Looting, revenge killing and subversive activities are rife ... Should a bloody and protracted insurgency establish itself in Baghdad, then a ripple effect is likely to occur."[234]

652. Gen Jackson recognised that the UK's ability to maintain the consent of the population in the South depended on a stable and secure Baghdad, and advised:

> "The bottom line is that if we choose not to influence Baghdad we must be confident of the US ability to improve [its tactics] before tolerance is lost and insurgency sets in."

653. Gen Jackson, Major General David Richards (Assistant Chief of the General Staff) and Lieutenant General Sir Anthony Pigott (Deputy Chief of the Defence Staff (Commitments)) all offered advice in favour of deploying the UK's 16 Air Assault Brigade to Baghdad to support Coalition efforts to retrain Iraqi police officers and get them back on patrol.

654. However, the Chiefs of Staff collectively considered that the benefits of making a contribution to the security of Baghdad were outweighed by the risk that UK troops would be "tied down" outside the UK's Area of Responsibility, with adverse impact, and

---

[233] Telegram 359 IraqRep to FCO London, 28 June 2004, 'Iraq: Valedictory: The End of Occupation'.
[234] Minute CGS to CDS, 13 May 2003, 'CGS Visit to Op. TELIC 7-10 May 2003'.

advised on 21 May against deploying 16 Air Assault Brigade. The Chiefs of Staff did not conclude that the tasks it was proposed that 16 Air Assault Brigade should undertake were unnecessary, but rather that US troops would complete them.

UK INFLUENCE ON POST-INVASION STRATEGY: RESOLUTION 1483

655. On 21 March 2003, the day after the start of the invasion, Mr Powell and Sir David Manning, two of Mr Blair's closest advisers, offered him advice on how to influence the post-invasion US agenda. Key among their concerns was the need for post-conflict administrative arrangements to have the legitimacy conferred by UN endorsement. Such UK plans for the post-conflict period as had been developed relied on the deployment of an international reconstruction effort to Iraq. Controversy surrounding the launch of the invasion made that challenging to deliver; the absence of UN endorsement would make it close to impossible.

656. Discussion between the US and UK on the content of a new UN Security Council resolution began the same day. Resolution 1483 (2003) was eventually adopted on 22 May.

657. US and UK objectives for the resolution were different, and in several substantive respects the text of resolution 1483 differed from the UK's preferred position.

658. The UK wanted oil revenues to be controlled by an Iraqi body, or failing that by the UN or World Bank, in line with the pre-invasion promise to use them exclusively for the benefit of Iraq. Instead, resolution 1483 placed the power to spend the Development Fund for Iraq into the hands of the Coalition Provisional Authority (CPA), overseen by a monitoring board. That was in line with US objectives, but did not address UK concerns.

659. The UK considered that an Interim Iraqi Administration should have real powers, and not be subordinate to the CPA. Resolution 1483 said that the CPA would retain its responsibilities until an internationally recognised representative government was established. The text did not go so far as to require an interim administration to report formally to the CPA, as the US wished, but that was in effect how the relationship between the CPA and the Governing Council established by resolution 1483 operated.

660. The UK's policy position was that the UN should take the lead in establishing the Interim Iraqi Administration. Resolution 1483 gave the UN a role working with the people of Iraq and the CPA, but did not give it the lead. Evidence considered by the Inquiry suggests that there was consistent reluctance on the part of the UN to take on such a role and the UK position was therefore not wholly realistic.

661. Resolution 1483 formally designated the UK and US as joint Occupying Powers in Iraq. It also set the conditions for the CPA's dominance over post-invasion strategy and policy by handing it control of funding for reconstruction and influence on political development at least equal to that of the UN.

UK INFLUENCE ON THE COALITION PROVISIONAL AUTHORITY

662. By the time resolution 1483 was adopted, the CPA was already operating in Iraq under the leadership of Ambassador L Paul Bremer, reporting to Mr Donald Rumsfeld, the US Defense Secretary. There was no reporting line from the CPA to the UK.

663. The resolution's designation of the US and UK as joint Occupying Powers did not reflect the reality of the Occupation. The UK contribution to the CPA's effort was much smaller than that of the US and was particularly concerned with Basra.

664. The UK took an early decision to concentrate its effort in one geographical area rather than accept a national lead for a particular element of the Coalition effort (such as police reform). However, it was inevitable that Iraq's future would be determined in Baghdad, as both the administrative centre and the place where the power shift from minority Sunni rule to majority Shia rule was going to be most keenly felt. Having decided to concentrate its effort on an area some distance removed from the capital, the UK's ability to influence policy under debate in Baghdad was curtailed.

665. In Baghdad itself, the UK provided only a small proportion of the staff for the military and civilian headquarters. The low numbers were influenced in part by reasonable concerns about the personal legal liabilities of UK staff working initially in ORHA and then in the CPA, and what their deployment might imply about the UK's responsibility for decisions made by those organisations, in the absence of formal consultation or the right of veto.

666. The pre-invasion focus on a leading UN role in Iraq meant that little thought had been given to the status of UK personnel during an occupation which followed an invasion without Security Council authorisation. Better planning, including proper assessment of a variety of different possible scenarios, would have allowed such issues to be worked through at a much earlier stage.

667. There was an urgent need for suitably experienced UK officials ready to deploy to Baghdad, but they had not been identified (see Section 15).

668. No governance arrangements were designed before the invasion which might have enabled officials and Ministers based in London and Washington to manage the implications of a joint occupation involving separate resources of a very different scale. Such arrangements would have provided a means to identify and resolve different perspectives on policy, and to facilitate joint decisions.

669. Once the CPA had been established, policy decisions were made largely in Baghdad, where there was also no formal US/UK governance structure. This created a risk described to the Inquiry by Sir Michael Wood, FCO Legal Adviser from 2001 to 2006, as "the UK being held jointly responsible for acts or omissions of the CPA, without a right to consult and a right of joint decision".[235]

---

[235] Statement, 15 March 2011, page 22.

670. To manage that risk, the UK proposed a Memorandum of Understanding (MOU) with the US to establish procedures for working together on issues related to the Occupation, but it could not be agreed. Having supplied the overwhelming majority of the CPA's resources, the US had little incentive to give the UK an influential role in deciding how those resources were to be used, and the UK lacked the will and leverage to insist.

671. In the absence of formal arrangements, there was a clear risk that the UK would be inadequately involved in important decisions, and the UK struggled from the start to have a significant effect on the CPA's policies. This was a source of concern to both Ministers and officials in 2003, but the issue was never resolved.

672. Senior individuals deployed to Iraq by the UK at this time saw themselves either as working for the CPA in support of its objectives and as part of its chain of command, or as UK representatives within the CPA with a remit to seek to influence CPA decisions. No-one formally represented the UK position within the CPA decision-making process, a serious weakness which should have been addressed at an early stage.

673. Managing a joint occupation of such size and complexity effectively and coherently required regular formal and informal discussion and clear decision-making at all levels, both between capitals and in-country. Once attempts to agree an MOU had failed, the chances of constructing such mechanisms were slim.

674. In the absence of an MOU with the US, the UK's influence in Baghdad depended heavily on the personal impact of successive Special Representatives and British Ambassadors to Iraq and the relationships they were able to build with senior US figures.

675. Some instances of important CPA decisions in which the UK played little or no formal part were:

- The decision to issue CPA Order No.2, which "dissolved" (or disbanded) a number of military and other security entities that had operated as part of Saddam Hussein's regime, including the armed forces (see Section 12). This was raised informally by Ambassador Bremer in his first meeting with Mr John Sawers, Mr Blair's Special Representative on Iraq, who – unbriefed – did not at that point take a contrary position. The concept of creating a new army had also been raised by Mr Walt Slocombe, CPA Senior Adviser on National Security and Defense, in discussion with Mr Hoon. Dissolution was a key decision which was to have a significant effect on the alienation of the Sunni community and the development of an insurgency in Iraq, and the terms and timing of this important Order should have been approved by both Washington and London.

- Decisions on how to spend the Development Fund for Iraq, which resolution 1483 gave the CPA the power to make. CPA Regulation No.2 subsequently vested Ambassador Bremer with control of the Fund, effectively placing it under US control. This exacerbated concerns about the under-resourcing of CPA(South) as expressed in Mr Straw's letter to Mr Blair of 5 June 2003 (see Section 10.1).

- The creation of the Iraqi Central Bank as an independent body in July 2003 (see Sections 9.2 and 10.1). This came as a surprise to the UK despite the close involvement of officials from the Treasury in arrangements for Iraq's new currency and budget.

- The creation of a new Iraqi Central Criminal Court (see Section 9.2), the announcement of which UK officials could not delay for long enough to enable the Attorney General to give his view on its legality under the terms of resolution 1483.

- Production of the CPA's 'Vision for Iraq' and 'Achieving the Vision' (see Sections 9.2 and 10.1). Mr Sawers alerted the FCO to the first document on 6 July when it was already at an advanced stage of drafting, and by 18 July it had been signed off by the Pentagon. No formal UK approval was sought for a document which was intended to provide strategic direction to the Coalition's non-military effort in Iraq.

676. UK involvement in CPA decisions about the scope and implementation of de-Ba'athification policy is considered in Section 11.2.

677. In some areas, the UK was able to affect CPA policy through the influence that Mr Sawers or his successor Sir Jeremy Greenstock exerted on senior US officials. Both used their diplomatic experience to build connections with Iraqi politicians and contribute to the political development of Iraq. Instances of UK influence included:

- Mr Sawers' involvement in the plans for an Interim Iraqi Administration, in respect of which he considered that "much of the thinking is ours".[236]

- Sir Jeremy Greenstock's "two chickens, two eggs" plan, which overcame political stalemate between the CPA and Grand Ayatollah al-Sistani on how the new Iraqi Constitution should be created. The plan led to the 15 November Agreement which set the timetable for transfer of sovereignty to a transitional administration by 30 June 2004.

- Ensuring that negotiations on the content of the Transitional Administrative Law reached a successful conclusion. Sir Jeremy Greenstock told the Inquiry that he had prevented the Kurdish delegation from leaving, "which Bremer wasn't aware of".[237]

---

[236] Telegram 028 IraqRep to FCO London, 1 June 2003, 'Iraq: Political Process'.
[237] Private hearing, 26 May 2010, page 64.

- The level of female representation in Iraq's new political structures, including the 25 percent "goal" for members of the National Assembly set by the Transitional Administrative Law, which the UK pursued with some success.

678. In the absence of decision-making arrangements in which the UK had a formal role, too much reliance was placed on communication between Mr Blair and President Bush, one of the very small number of ways of influencing US policy. Some issues were addressed by this route: for instance, using his regular conversations with President Bush, Mr Blair was able, with some success, to urge caution in relation to the US operation in Fallujah in April 2004.

679. But the channel of communication between Prime Minister and President should be reserved for the most strategic and most intractable issues. It is not the right mechanism for day-to-day policy-making or an effective way of making tactical decisions.

680. It is impossible to say whether a greater and more formal UK input to CPA decisions would have led to better outcomes. But it is clear that the UK's ability to influence decisions made by the CPA was not commensurate with its responsibilities as joint Occupying Power.

A DECLINE IN SECURITY

681. From early June 2003, and throughout the summer, there were signs that security in both Baghdad and the South was deteriorating. The MOD's SPG warned that "more organised opposition to the Coalition may be emerging"[238] as discontent about the Coalition's failure to deliver a secure environment began to grow in the Iraqi population.

682. The extent of the decline in Baghdad and central Iraq overshadowed the decline in Multi-National Division (South-East) (MND(SE)). Food shortages and the failure of essential services such as the supply of electricity and water, plus lack of progress in the political process, however, began to erode the relationship between UK forces and the local population. The deterioration was exemplified by attacks on UK forces in Majar al-Kabir in Maysan province on 22 and 24 June.

683. As the summer wore on, authoritative sources in the UK, such as the JIC, began to identify issues with the potential to escalate into conflict and to recognise the likelihood that extremist groups would become more co-ordinated. The constraint imposed on reconstruction activities by the lack of security began to be apparent. Mr Sawers and Sir David Manning expressed concern about whether the UK had sufficient troops deployed in MND(SE), and about the permeability of Maysan's substantial border with Iran.

---

[238] Minute SECCOS to PSO/CDS, 10 June 2003, 'OP COS Paper: UK Contribution to Iraq: Strategic Intent and Direction' attaching Paper SPG, 9 June 2003, 'UK contribution to Iraq: strategic intent and direction'.

684. From early July, security was seen in Whitehall as the key concern and was raised by Mr Blair with President Bush.

685. A circular analysis began to develop, in which progress on reconstruction required security to be improved, and improved security required the consent generated by reconstruction activity. Lieutenant General Robert Fry, Deputy Chief of the Defence Staff (Commitments), reported "a decline in Iraqi consent to the Coalition in MND(SE) due to the failure by the Coalition to deliver improvements in essential services" and that Shia leaders were warning of a short grace period before further significant deterioration.

686. By the autumn of 2003, violence was escalating in Baghdad and attacks were becoming more sophisticated. Attacks on the UN in August and September, which injured and killed a number of UN officials including the UN Special Representative for Iraq, prompted some organisations to withdraw their international staff. Although Basra was less turbulent than the capital, the risk of a ripple effect from Baghdad – as identified by Gen Jackson in May – remained.

687. The JIC assessed on 3 September that the security environment would probably worsen over the year ahead. There had been a number of serious attacks on the Coalition in MND(SE), and Islamic "extremists/terrorists"[239] were expected to remain a long-term threat in Iraq. The UK's military and civilian representatives on the ground were reporting a growing insurgency in central Iraq.

688. Despite that evidence, military planning under the leadership of General Sir Michael Walker, Chief of the Defence Staff, proceeded on the basis that the situation in Basra would remain relatively benign.

689. The Inquiry considers that a deterioration in security could and should have been identified by Lt Gen Reith by the end of August 2003 and that the cumulative evidence of a deteriorating security situation should have led him to conclude that the underlying assumptions on which the UK's Iraq campaign was based was over-optimistic, and to instigate a review of the scale of the UK's military effort in Iraq.

690. There were a number of issues that might have been examined by such a review, including:

- whether the UK had sufficient resources in MND(SE) to deal with a worsening security situation; and
- whether the UK should engage outside MND(SE) in the interests of Iraq's overall stability (as had been advocated by Gen Jackson, Maj Gen Richards and Lt Gen Pigott).

691. No such review took place.

---

[239] JIC Assessment, 3 September 2003, 'Iraq: Threats to Security'.

692. There was a strong case for reinforcing MND(SE) so that it could handle its high-priority tasks (providing essential security for reconstruction projects, protecting existing infrastructure, guarding key sites and improving border security to inhibit the import of arms from Iran) effectively in changing circumstances. Those tasks all demanded a higher level of manpower than was available. Although additional military personnel were deployed in September 2003, mainly to fill existing gaps in support for reconstruction activities, their numbers were far too small to have a significant impact.

693. The failure to consider the option of reinforcement at this time was a serious omission and Lt Gen Reith and Gen Walker should have ensured that UK force levels in MND(SE) were formally reconsidered in autumn 2003 or at the latest by the end of the year. Increases in UK force levels in order to address the security situation should have been recommended to Ministers. Any opportunity to regain the initiative and pre-empt further deterioration in the security situation was lost.

694. In October, Sir Jeremy Greenstock reported that Lieutenant General Ricardo Sanchez, Commander Combined Joint Task Force-7, had "come to recognise that Coalition operations are at a standstill and that there is a need to regain momentum".[240] Doubts started to build about the chances of credible elections based on a legitimate constitution in the course of 2004 and work began to look for alternatives to the plan set out by Ambassador Bremer. The "bloodiest 48-hour period in Baghdad since March",[241] including an attack on the al-Rashid Hotel in Baghdad's Green Zone, was sufficient to convince some that a pivotal point in the security situation had been reached.

695. When President Bush visited London in November, Mr Blair provided him with a paper written by Sir Jeremy Greenstock which argued that security should be the highest priority in the run-up to June 2004, when the Iraqi Transitional Government would take power. Sir Jeremy suggested that troop levels should be looked at again and highlighted "the dangers we face if we do not get a grip on the security situation" as a topic that President Bush and Mr Blair needed to discuss in stark terms.

696. The constraints within which the UK was operating as a result of the limited scale of forces deployed in Iraq were articulated clearly for the Chiefs of Staff in December. Lt Gen Fry argued that a strategy of "early effect"[242] was needed which prioritised campaign success. Operation TELIC was the UK "Main Effort", but deploying additional resources in a way that was compliant with the Defence Planning Assumptions would require the withdrawal of resources from other operations.

697. On 1 January 2004, Sir Jeremy Greenstock wrote bluntly: "This theatre remains a security crisis."[243]

---

[240] Telegram 230 IraqRep to FCO London, 24 October 2003, 'Iraq: Security Update'.
[241] Telegram 1426 Washington to FCO London, 28 October 2003, 'Iraq: US Views 28 October'.
[242] Minute DCDS(C) to COSSEC, 5 December 2003, 'Op TELIC – Review of UK Military Strategy for Iraq'.
[243] Telegram 337 IraqRep to FCO London, 1 January 2004, 'Iraq: Six Final Months of Occupation'.

698. Despite mounting evidence of violent insurgency, the UK's policy of military drawdown in Iraq continued. After force levels had been reviewed in January, the rationale for continued drawdown was based on adjusted criteria by which the success of Security Sector Reform would be judged, meaning that such reform would be implemented "only to applicable standards for Iraq".[244]

THE TURNING POINT

699. February 2004 was the worst month for Coalition casualties since the fall of Saddam Hussein's regime. More than 200 people, mainly Iraqi citizens, were killed in suicide attacks. Attacks on the Iraqi Security Forces were increasing and concerns about Islamic extremists operating in Iraq began to grow. By the end of March, more than 200 attacks targeting Iraqi citizens were being reported each week.

700. In April, there was a sudden escalation in attacks by the Jaysh al-Mahdi (JAM) in Basra, described by the General Officer Commanding MND(SE) as "like a switch had been flicked".[245] In Fallujah, a US offensive which followed the ambush and murder of four security contractors provoked an angry response from the Sunni community.

701. The significant worsening of security, coupled with revelations of abuse by members of the US military of Iraqi detainees held in Abu Ghraib prison, led many of the Inquiry's witnesses to conclude that the spring of 2004 had been a turning point.

702. At the end of April, Mr Blair's analysis was that the key issue in Iraq was not multi-faceted, rather it was "simple: security".[246]

703. Despite the failing security situation in MND(SE) in spring 2004, Gen Walker was explicit that no additional troops were required for the tasks currently assigned to the UK.

704. The Chiefs of Staff maintained the view they had originally reached in November 2003, that HQ Allied Rapid Reaction Corps (ARRC) should not be actively considered for deployment to Iraq, even though:

- Iraq was a higher priority for the UK than Afghanistan;
- security in Iraq was clearly worsening and had been identified by Mr Blair as the key issue; and
- there had been a specific US request for deployment of HQ ARRC.

---

[244] Minute Reith to PSO/CDS, 29 January 2004, 'Op TELIC Force Level Review – Jan 04'.
[245] Public hearing Lamb, 9 December 2009, pages 67-68.
[246] Letter Rycroft to Owen, 26 April 2004, 'Iraq: 15 Reports for the Prime Minister'.

Transition

UK INFLUENCE ON US STRATEGY POST-CPA

705. In June 2004, the US and UK ceased to be Occupying Powers in Iraq and the CPA was disbanded. Responsibility for day-to-day interaction on civil affairs with the Iraqi Interim Government on civil affairs passed to the newly appointed British and US Ambassadors.

706. After the handover, the UK's priorities were to maintain the momentum of the political process towards elections in January 2005, and to ensure that the conditions for the drawdown of its forces were achieved.

707. Mr Blair and President Bush continued to discuss Iraq on a regular basis. It continued to be the case that relatively small issues were raised to this level. The UK took false comfort that it was involved in US decision-making from the strength of that relationship.

708. Themes which Mr Blair emphasised to President Bush included the acceleration of Security Sector Reform and the Iraqiisation of security, UN engagement, better outreach to the Sunni community (often referred to as "reconciliation"), provision of direct support to Prime Minister Ayad Allawi and better use of local media to transmit a positive message about the coalition's intentions and actions.

PLANNING FOR WITHDRAWAL

709. By July 2004, the UK envisaged that, providing the necessary criteria were met, there would be a gradual reduction in troop numbers during 2005 leading to final withdrawal in 2006, to be followed by a period of "Strategic Overwatch".

710. The most important of the criteria that would enable coalition troops to withdraw was the ability of the Iraqi Security Forces to take the lead on security (Iraqiisation). Having recognised that a stable and secure environment was the key factor on which progress in Iraq depended, by May 2004 the UK solution was "a better and quicker plan for building Iraqi capacity in the Police, Civil Defence Corps, the Army and the Intelligence Service".[247] This made sense in the long term but was unlikely to meet the requirement to regain control of Iraq rapidly in the face of a mounting insurgency. Reform of the Iraqi Security Forces is addressed in detail in Section 12.

711. By mid-August, the level of attacks against coalition forces had matched the previous peak in April of the same year. In September, Lieutenant General John McColl (Senior British Military Representative – Iraq) judged that the Iraqi Security Forces would not be able to take full responsibility for security before 2006.

---

[247] Letter Bowen to Baker, 13 May 2004, 'Iraq: Security'.

712. In September 2004, Gen Walker received a well-argued piece of advice from Lt Gen McColl which made clear that the conditions on which decisions on drawdown were to be based were unlikely to be met in the near future. Despite the warnings in Lt Gen McColl's paper and his advice that "the time is right for the consideration of the substantive issues",[248] the Chiefs of Staff, chaired by Gen Walker, declined to engage in a substantive review of UK options.

713. The Inquiry recognises that the scale of the resources which the UK might have deployed to deal with the issues was substantially less than the US could bring to bear. It is possible that the UK may not have been able to make a real difference, when the key strategic change that might have affected the outcome was the deployment of a much larger force. But proper consideration ought to have been given to what options were available, including for the deployment of additional personnel. Mr Straw raised the need for such a debate with Mr Blair in October.

714. The UK had consistently resisted US requests to deploy additional personnel, which Lt Gen McColl described as having "chipped away at the US/UK relationship",[249] but in October it was agreed that the Black Watch would be deployed to North Babil for 30 days to backfill US forces needed for operations in Fallujah. Approximately 350 personnel from 1st Battalion, the Royal Highland Fusiliers were also deployed to Iraq to provide additional security across MND(SE) during the election period in January and February 2005. The UK remained reluctant to commit any further forces in the longer term: when Dutch forces withdrew from Muthanna province, the UK instead redeployed forces from elsewhere in MND(SE) plus a small amount of additional logistic support.

715. In January 2005, Lt Gen Fry produced a thoughtful and realistic assessment of the prospects for security in Iraq, observing that "we are not on track to deliver the Steady State Criteria (SSC) before the UN mandate expires, or even shortly thereafter".[250] He judged that "only additional military effort by the MNF-I [Multi-National Force – Iraq] as a whole" might be able to get the campaign back on track. Lt Gen Fry identified three possible courses of action for the UK: increasing the UK scale of effort, maintaining the status quo or, if it were judged that the campaign was irretrievable, accepting failure and seeking to mitigate UK liability.

716. The Inquiry endorses Lt Gen Fry's assessment of the options open to the UK at this point and considers that full and proper consideration should have been given to each option by DOP.

717. In his advice to Mr Blair on 21 January, Gen Walker did not expose the assessment made by Lt Gen Fry that only additional military effort by the MNF-I might be able to get the campaign back on track.

---

[248] Minute McColl to CDS and CJO, 26 September 2004, 'Report 130 of 26 Sep 04'.
[249] Report McColl to CDS and CJO, 20 October 2004, 'SBMR-I Hauldown Report – Lt Gen McColl'.
[250] Minute DCDS(C) to APS 2/SofS [MOD], 11 January 2005, 'Iraq 2005 – a UK MOD perspective'.

718. On 30 January, elections for the Transitional National Assembly and Provincial Assemblies took place across Iraq. Security arrangements involved 130,000 personnel from the Iraqi Security Forces, supported by 184,500 troops from the MNF-I. The JIC assessed that perhaps fewer than 10 percent of voters had turned out in the Sunni heartlands and judged that "without Sunni engagement in the political process, it will not be possible significantly to undermine the insurgency".

719. In April, the JIC assessed that:

> "A significant Sunni insurgency will continue through 2005 and beyond, but the opportunities for reducing it appear greater than we judged in early February."[251]

THE IMPACT OF AFGHANISTAN

720. In June 2004, the UK had made a public commitment to deploy HQ ARRC to Afghanistan in 2006, based on a recommendation from the Chiefs of Staff and Mr Hoon, and with Mr Straw's support. HQ ARRC was a NATO asset for which the UK was the lead nation and provided 60 percent of its staff.

721. It appears that senior members of the Armed Forces reached the view, throughout 2004 and 2005, that little more would be achieved in MND(SE) and that it would make more sense to concentrate military effort on Afghanistan where it might have greater effect.

722. In February 2005, the UK announced that it would switch its existing military effort in Afghanistan from the north to Helmand province in the south.

723. In 2002, *A New Chapter*, an MOD review of the 1998 *Strategic Defence Review* (SDR), had reaffirmed that the UK's Armed Forces would be unable to support two enduring medium scale military operations at the same time:

> "Since the SDR we have assumed that we should plan to be able to undertake either a single major operation (of a similar scale and duration to our contribution to the Gulf War in 1990-91), or undertake a more extended overseas deployment on a lesser scale (as in the mid-1990s in Bosnia), while retaining the ability to mount a second substantial deployment ... if this were made necessary by a second crisis. We would not, however, expect both deployments to involve war-fighting or to maintain them simultaneously for longer than six months."[252]

724. As described in Section 16.1, since 2002 the Armed Forces had been consistently operating at or above the level of concurrency defined in the 1998 SDR, and the continuation of Op TELIC had placed additional strain on military personnel.

---

[251] JIC Assessment, 6 April 2005, 'Iraq: The State of the Insurgency'.
[252] Ministry of Defence, *Strategic Defence Review: A New Chapter*, July 2002, page 14.

725. By May 2005, the UK had been supporting an operation of at least medium scale in Iraq for more than two years. The Ministerial Committee on Defence and Overseas Policy Sub-Committee on Iraq (DOP(I)) recognised that future force levels in Iraq would need to be considered in the context of the requirement to achieve "strategic balance" with commitments in Afghanistan, to ensure that both were properly resourced.

726. In July 2005, DOP agreed proposals for both the transfer of the four provinces in MND(SE) to Iraqi control and for the deployment of the UK Provincial Reconstruction Team then based in northern Afghanistan to Helmand province in the South, along with an infantry battlegroup and full helicopter support – around 2,500 personnel.

727. As described under the heading 'Iraqiisation' below, the proposals to transfer responsibility for security in the four provinces of MND(SE) to Iraqi control were based on high-risk assumptions about the capability of the Iraqi Security Forces to take the lead for security. If those assumptions proved to be inaccurate and the UK was unable to withdraw, agreement to the Helmand deployment in Afghanistan effectively constrained the UK's ability to respond by increasing troop levels in Iraq.

728. In January 2006, Cabinet approved the decision to deploy to Helmand. Dr Reid, the Defence Secretary, announced that the UK was "preparing for a deployment to southern Afghanistan" which included a Provincial Reconstruction Team as "part of a larger, more than 3,300-strong British force providing the security framework".[253]

729. The impact of that decision was summarised neatly by Gen Walker as:

> "Militarily, the UK force structure is already stretched and, with two concurrent medium scale operations in prospect, will soon become exceptionally so in niche areas."[254]

730. Niche capabilities such as helicopter support and Intelligence, Surveillance, Target Acquisition and Reconnaissance (ISTAR) were essential to the successful conduct of operations.

731. From July 2005 onwards, decisions in relation to resources for Iraq were effectively made under the influence of the demands of the UK effort in Afghanistan. Although Iraq remained the stated UK main effort, the Government no longer had the option of a substantial reinforcement of its forces there, should it have considered one necessary. When the US announced in January 2007 that it would send a surge of resources to Iraq, the UK was consequently unable to contemplate a parallel surge of its own.

732. The impact of the decision to deploy to Helmand on the availability of key equipment capabilities for Iraq, and on the level of stretch felt by military personnel, is addressed in Sections 14 and 16.

---

[253] House of Commons, *Official Report,* 26 January 2006, columns 1529-1533.
[254] Letter Walker to Richards, 24 January 2006, [untitled].

IRAQIISATION

733. After becoming Defence Secretary in May 2005, Dr Reid had continued the policy of reducing UK troop levels based on the transition of lead responsibility for security to the Iraqi Security Forces (ISF). In one of his early acts as Defence Secretary, he announced the deployment of just over 400 additional personnel to enhance the UK's effort in training the ISF, which would "enable them to take on ever greater responsibility for their own security and so pave the way for UK troops to withdraw".[255]

734. The proposals for transfer of the four provinces in MND(SE) to Iraqi control agreed in July 2005 suggested transition from MNF-I to ISF primacy in Basra from March 2006, based on the assumption that the ISF would, by that point, be capable of taking on responsibility for security in what was likely to remain a very challenging environment.

735. There was sufficient reliable contemporary evidence available, including from the JIC and in reports from commanders in theatre, to demonstrate that the assumption that the ISF would be ready to take the lead in Basra by that point was probably unrealistic.

736. In September 2005, Mr Blair expressed his concerns about ISF capability, following reports of police involvement in attacks on the MNF in Basra. But despite concerns that had been expressed about the capacity of the ISF, Dr Reid recommended that a reduction in UK forces should take place in October or November 2005.

737. A few days after Dr Reid made his recommendation, the Jameat incident in Basra (see Section 12.1) raised questions about the ISF in MND(SE). Officials from the FCO, the MOD and DFID judged that the incident had highlighted the risks to achieving UK objectives in MND(SE), and that those risks had implications for military resources. Nevertheless, assumptions about ISF readiness were not re-examined by Ministers. The incident should have prompted a more searching analysis of whether the conditions necessary for drawdown were likely to be met within the planned timetable. Reluctance to consider the potential implications of the Jameat incident obscured what it had revealed about the security situation in MND(SE).

738. The critical importance of ISF capability in assessing readiness for transfer to Provincial Iraqi Control, on which UK plans to draw down were based, was emphasised by the 'Conditions for Provincial Transfer' published by the Joint Iraqi/MNF Committee to Transfer Security Responsibility, and by Dr Reid, who told DOP(I) that "successful Iraqiisation remains the key".[256] DOP(I) decided that Dr Reid should have lead responsibility for building the capacity of the Iraqi Police Service (IPS) in Basra in addition to his responsibility for the Iraqi Army.

739. In October 2005, Mr Blair asked for a major and sustained push to make progress on the ability of the ISF to take the lead on security. Gen Jackson raised concerns about ISF effectiveness in a minute to Gen Walker, and concluded: "it is not to our credit that

---

[255] House of Commons, *Official Report*, 25 May 2005, column 15WS.
[256] Paper Reid, 11 October 2005, 'Iraq: Security Update'.

we have known about the inadequacies of the IPS for so long and yet failed to address them".[257] The Assessments Staff reinforced the lack of progress in reforming the ISF.

740. In October 2005, the Chiefs of Staff made a stark assessment of the insurgency and coalition strategy in Iraq. They concluded that "Ministers needed to be clear that the campaign could potentially be heading for 'strategic failure', with grave national and international consequences if the appropriate actions were not taken".[258] Gen Walker judged that only 5 percent of UK military effort in MND(SE) was devoted to counter-insurgency operations. But neither Air Marshal Sir Glenn Torpy, Commander Joint Operations, nor Gen Walker reassessed UK force requirements in Iraq, based on those two assessments.

741. The security situation at this point should have resulted in a reassessment of the UK troop levels needed to achieve the UK's key outcomes in MND(SE). Although the responsibility for tactical decision-making rested with commanders on the ground, it was for Gen Walker to ensure that those commanders had sufficient resources to deliver.

742. The absence of additional resources placed further pressure on the UK's ability to deliver the conditions required for transfer. At the end of 2005 and in early 2006 there were further indications that the ISF were not ready to operate alone. The MOD reported to the final DOP(I) meeting of 2005 that the capacity of the Iraqi administration and security forces to assume responsibility, acknowledging the challenge of increasing sectarianism and militia infiltration, was one of the key challenges remaining.

743. In March 2006, the JIC again highlighted doubts about the ability of the Iraqi Army to operate without MNF support and concerns about the corruption and infiltration of the IPS.

744. US concerns about UK plans for the transition of Maysan and Muthanna to Iraqi control in May were such that Dr Reid adapted them to include a small residual team providing mentoring and support to the Iraqi Army.

745. Dr Reid continued to press ahead with drawdown and announced that troop levels would reduce in May 2006 from approximately 8,000 to around 7,200 based on "completion of various security sector reform tasks, a reduction in the support levels for those tasks, and recent efficiency measures in theatre".[259] That rationale did not include an assessment of the effect of those tasks on the capability of the ISF.

---

[257] Minute CGS to CDS, 18 October 2005, 'CGS visit to Iraq: 10-13 Oct 05'.
[258] Minutes, 18 October 2005, Chiefs of Staff meeting.
[259] Letter Reid to Blair, 9 March 2006, 'Iraq: Force Level Review and Announcement'.

Preparation for withdrawal

A MAJOR DIVERGENCE IN STRATEGY

746. US and UK strategies for Iraq had in effect been on different courses since the UK decision to focus its attention on MND(SE) in 2003. As a result of that decision, the UK had acquired distinctly different priorities from the US. It was only marginally involved in the central tasks of stabilising the Iraqi Government in Baghdad and managing sectarian divisions, while it had come to see its main task in Basra as one of keeping the situation calm while building the case for drawdown.

747. For some time, there had been indications of tension between the US and UK regarding assessments of progress, and differing assumptions about whether plans were needed for long-term bases in Iraq. In May 2006, Mr Blair was told about "rumblings from the US system about UK failure to grip the security situation in what they regard as a strategically vital part of Iraq".[260] Gen Jackson felt compelled to report that:

> "The perception, right or wrong, in some – if not all – US military circles is that the UK is motivated more by the short-term political gain of early withdrawal than by the long-term importance of mission accomplishment; and that, as a result, MND(SE)'s operational posture is too laissez faire and lacks initiative ..."[261]

748. In January 2007, the divergence between US and UK strategies was thrown into sharp relief by President Bush's announcement that the US would adopt a new strategy, of which a prominent feature would be the deployment of a surge of US forces, primarily to Baghdad and its environs. UK assessments of the prospects for the new US policy were bleak, reflecting widespread pessimism about the prospects for Iraq. UK strategy continued to look towards withdrawal.

749. US concerns about the differences in approach were evident. In February 2007, Sir David Manning, British Ambassador to the US, reported that Secretary Rice had asked him "to tell her honestly whether the UK was now making for the exit as fast as possible".[262]

750. The divergence in strategies was also illustrated by the conditions-based process through which the four provinces in MND(SE) were transferred to Provincial Iraqi Control (PIC) during 2007. Although each transfer was signed off by senior members of the US military, there was persistent reporting of US concerns about readiness for PIC, whether the conditions had actually been met and the wider impact of transfer.

751. The US was also uncomfortable about arrangements made by the UK with a militia group in Basra which allowed the safe exit of UK troops from their main base in the city.

---

[260] Minute Phillipson to Prime Minister, 2 May 2006, 'VTC with President Bush, 1615 2 May 2006'.
[261] Minute CGS to CDS, 22 May 2006, 'CGS visit to Iraq: 15-18 May 06'.
[262] Letter Manning to Hayes, 1 February 2007, 'Conversation with the US Secretary of State, 31 January 2007'.

A POSSIBLE CIVIL WAR

752. By March 2006, senior members of the UK military were considering the possibility of civil war in Iraq, prompted by rising levels of sectarian violence and concerns that the Iraqi Government was "not ... perceived as even-handed in security issues".[263] The risk of civil war had been acknowledged by Prime Minister Ibrahim Ja'afari in the wake of the bombing of the al-Askari mosque in February. Although there was general agreement that the situation in Iraq did not constitute civil war, the risk that one might develop was considered to be real.

753. At this time, the presence in Iraq of the MNF was authorised by resolution 1637 (2005). The exchange of letters between Prime Minister Ja'afari and the President of the Security Council which accompanied the resolution clearly identified providing security for the Iraqi people as the reason why a continued MNF presence was necessary.

754. In late April, FCO officials were concerned that security in Basra was declining and that a determined and sustained effort, including a more assertive military posture, would be required to deliver the UK's objective of transferring Basra to Iraqi control by late 2006 or early 2007.

755. Accounts from mid-2006 suggested that security in MND(SE) was a significant concern, characterised by "steady, if generally unspectacular, decline"[264] and increased militia activity. The UK military's approach had generated US concern and the security situation was limiting UK civilian activity.

756. Gen Jackson's assessment in May of the short-term security prospects in Iraq was bleak. He judged that "what we will leave behind will not look much like strategic success. Ten years hence our strategy may fully bear fruit."[265]

757. After visiting Iraq in early May, Air Chief Marshal Sir Jock Stirrup, Chief of the Defence Staff, advised Dr Reid that there should be no change to the operational approach and that there were "compelling reasons" why the UK should "press on" with handing over security to Iraq, including to permit the UK's continuing build-up in Afghanistan.[266] ACM Stirrup identified the risk that UK withdrawal from Basra would be seen as a "strategic failure" and suggested that "astute conditioning of the UK public may be necessary" to avoid that.

758. ACM Stirrup's view that the UK should press ahead with drawdown despite the security challenges in Basra was not consistent with Government policy that withdrawal should be conditions-based.

---

[263] Minute Houghton to CDS, 5 March 2006, 'SBMR-I Weekly Report (201) 5 March 06'.
[264] Minute senior government official specialising in the Middle East to Dowse, 12 May 2006, 'Situation in Basrah'.
[265] Minute CGS to CDS, 22 May 2006, 'CGS visit to Iraq: 15-18 May 06'.
[266] Minute Stirrup to SofS [MOD], 8 May 2006, 'CDS Visit to Iraq and Afghanistan – 5-7 May 06'.

759. ACM Stirrup's acceptance that the "law of diminishing returns" was "now firmly in play" and that there was "an increasing risk" that UK forces would "become part of the problem, rather than the solution" had some validity: it was clear from accounts of the situation in Basra that UK forces were not preventing a steady decline in security. ACM Stirrup was also right to advise Dr Reid that the MNF in Iraq faced a "multifaceted", sophisticated and dangerous enemy; that serious issues remained in Basra (militia activity, poor governance, insecurity); and that it was possible the UK would be accused of strategic failure.

760. The established policy was that UK forces would withdraw as the capabilities of the ISF increased until responsibility could be handed over to the Iraqi Government. ACM Stirrup's proposed remedy of continued drawdown and managing public opinion did not mitigate the risk of strategic failure he described.

761. In the summer of 2006, in recognition of the need to stabilise Basra and prepare it for transition to Iraqi control, the UK developed the Basra Security Plan, "a plan to improve Basra through operations, high impact reconstruction and SSR [Security Sector Reform] ... lasting for up to six months".[267] The military element of the plan became known as Operation SALAMANCA and included operations against militia groups.

762. In August 2006, ACM Stirrup was asked to give direction on both seeking US help for Op SALAMANCA and the possibility of deploying UK forces to support US operations outside MND(SE).

763. While ACM Stirrup stressed the importance of senior Iraqi political support if Op SALAMANCA was to be a success, Lieutenant General Nicholas Houghton, the Senior British Military Representative – Iraq, indicated a concern that even with US support the capabilities available in MND(SE) might not be sufficient successfully to deliver Op SALAMANCA.

764. ACM Stirrup directed that it was acceptable for the UK to make use of US enablers, such as aviation, in MND(SE), but that, in general, commitments in MND(SE) were to be met by existing MND(SE) personnel (including contractors) and any shortfalls were to be identified and considered appropriately.

765. ACM Stirrup also directed that the deployment of UK troops to Multi-National Division (Centre South):

> "... crossed a clear policy 'red line' and seemed counter-intuitive, given that consideration was also being given to obtaining US forces for MND(SE). The UK needed to draw down its force levels as soon as practicable, both in MND(SE) and elsewhere."[268]

---

[267] Minute Burke-Davies to APS/Secretary of State [MOD], 24 August 2006, 'Iraq: Op SALAMANCA'.
[268] Minutes, 2 August 2006, Chiefs of Staff meeting.

766. The decision not to allow the use of US support in Basra was an important one. The Inquiry considers that the question of what was needed to make Op SALAMANCA a success should have been addressed directly by ACM Stirrup, whose response instead precluded proper consideration of whether additional UK resources would be required.

767. There was continuing resistance to any suggestion that UK forces should operate outside MND(SE) and there may have been concern that US participation in Op SALAMANCA would have led to an obligation on the UK to engage more outside MND(SE). This might not, as ACM Stirrup observed, be consistent with a commitment to drawdown, but might have reduced the risk of strategic failure.

768. The nature of Op SALAMANCA was constrained by the Iraqi Government in September 2006, so that the eventual operation (renamed Operation SINBAD) left "Basra in the hands of the militant militia and death squads, with the ISF unable to impose, let alone maintain, the rule of law".[269] This contributed to the conditions which led the UK into negotiations with JAM in early 2007.

769. Attempts were subsequently made to present Op SINBAD as equivalent to the 2007 US surge. Although there was some resemblance between the "Clear, Hold, Build" tactics to be used by US surge forces and the UK's tactics for Op SINBAD, the UK operation did not deploy sufficient additional resources to conduct "Hold" and "Build" phases with anything like the same strategic effect. The additional 360 troops deployed by the UK could not have had the same effect as the more than 20,000 troops surged into Baghdad and its environs by the US.

770. At the end of 2006, tensions between the military and civilian teams in MND(SE) became explicit. In a report to Mr Blair, Major General Richard Shirreff, General Officer Commanding MND(SE), diagnosed that the existing arrangement, in which the Provincial Reconstruction Team was located in Kuwait, "lacks unity of command and unity of purpose"[270] and proposed the establishment of a "Joint Inter-Agency Task Force" in Basra led by the General Officer Commanding MND(SE).

771. ACM Stirrup's advice to Mr Blair was that it was "too late" to implement Maj Gen Shirreff's proposal. That may have been the right conclusion, but the effect was to deter consideration of a real problem and of ways in which military and civilian operations in MND(SE) could be better aligned.

772. The adequacy of UK force levels in Iraq and the effectiveness of the UK's efforts in MND(SE) were explicitly questioned in Maj Gen Shirreff's end of tour report.

---

[269] Minute Shirreff, 21 September 2006, 'GOC MND(SE) – Southern Iraq Update – 21 September 2006'.
[270] Letter Shirreff to Blair, 29 December 2006, [untitled].

FORCE LEVEL REVIEW

773. The balance of forces between Iraq and Afghanistan was reviewed by DOP in February 2007 on the basis that the UK could only sustain the enduring operational deployment of eight battlegroups.

774. ACM Stirrup's "strong advice",[271] with which DOP agreed, was that the UK should provide two additional battlegroups to the International Security Assistance Force in Afghanistan, reducing the Iraq to Afghanistan battlegroup ratio from 6:2 to 5:3 and then 4:4.

775. This advice did not include an assessment of either the actual state of security in Basra or the impact on the UK's ability to deliver its objectives (including that drawdown should be conditions-based) and responsibilities under resolution 1723 (2006). The advice did identify US "nervousness" about the UK proposals.

776. In early May, Sir Nigel Sheinwald, Mr Blair's Foreign Policy Adviser, sought ACM Stirrup's advice on the future of the UK military presence in Iraq. ACM Stirrup advised that the UK should press ahead with drawdown from Iraq on the basis that there was little more the UK could achieve. There was "no militarily useful mission".[272]

777. Mr Blair was concerned about the implications of ACM Stirrup's position unless the political circumstances in Basra changed first. He commented: "it will be <u>very</u> hard to present as anything other than a total withdrawal ... it cd be very dangerous for the stability of Iraq, & the US will, rightly, be v. concerned."[273]

778. After visiting Basra again in mid-May, ACM Stirrup continued to recommend the drawdown of UK forces. But other contemporary evidence indicated a more negative picture of circumstances in Basra than ACM Stirrup's view that:

> "... the Iraqis are increasingly in a position to take on responsibility for their own problems and therefore they might wish to look to propose the south of the country as a model through which we can recommend a drawdown of forces."[274]

779. In July 2007, FCO and MOD officials recognised that leaving Basra Palace would mean moving to PIC in fact if not in name. Mr Brown, who had become Prime Minister in June, was keen that the gap between leaving the Palace and transfer to PIC should be as small as possible, since UK situational awareness and ability to conduct operations in Basra would be limited once the Palace was no longer in use.

780. During a visit to Iraq at the start of July, ACM Stirrup sought to convince senior US officers that Basra was ready for transfer to PIC on the basis that it would not be possible to demonstrate readiness until after the transfer had taken place.

---

[271] Paper MOD officials, 13 February 2007, 'Iraq and Afghanistan: Balancing Military Effort in 2007'.
[272] Minute Sheinwald to Prime Minister, 3 May 2007, 'Iraq'.
[273] Manuscript comment Blair on Minute Sheinwald to Prime Minister, 3 May 2007, 'Iraq'.
[274] Minute Poffley to PSSC/SofS [MOD], 17 May 2007, 'CDS visit to Iraq 13-16 May 07'.

General David Petraeus, Commanding General MNF-I, and Ambassador Ryan Crocker, US Ambassador to Iraq, remained "circumspect" on the timing of PIC.[275] They considered that there remained "significant problems" associated with "unstable politics" and "JAM infiltration" in Basra.

781. As they reached the end of their respective tours of duty, both Major General Jonathan Shaw, General Officer Commanding MND(SE) from January to August 2007, and Lieutenant General William Rollo, Senior British Military Representative – Iraq from July 2007 to March 2008, identified the impact of limited resources on the UK's military effort and questioned the drive for continued drawdown in Iraq in order to prioritise resources for Helmand. Maj Gen Shaw wrote: "We have been hamstrung for resources throughout the tour, driven by the rising strategic significance of the Afghan deployment."[276]

782. During a visit to Iraq in October 2007, ACM Stirrup was briefed by Major General Graham Binns, General Office Commanding MND(SE) from August 2007 to February 2008, that the ISF might have only limited ability to cope in the event that JAM resumed combat operations. The JIC and others also identified continued weaknesses in the ISF. Their "ability and willingness to maintain security in the South remains patchy and dependent on MNF training, logistic and specialist air support".[277]

THE BEGINNING OF THE END

783. On 27 February 2008, the JIC assessed security prospects in the South at the request of the Permanent Joint Headquarters (PJHQ): security in Basra remained a concern.

784. In March 2008, Prime Minister Maliki instigated the Charge of the Knights to tackle militia groups in Basra. That such an important operation came as a surprise was an indication of the distance between the UK and Iraqi Governments at this point.

785. When the Charge of the Knights began, the UK found itself to be both compromised in the eyes of the Iraqi Government and unable to offer significant operational support, as a result of the tactical decision to negotiate with JAM1 and the absence of situational awareness in Basra after withdrawing from the Basra Palace site.

786. On 1 April, ACM Stirrup briefed the Overseas and Defence Sub-Committee of the National Security, International Relations and Development Committee (NSID(OD)) that the UK military task would be complete by the end of 2008; its timetable would not be affected by the Charge of the Knights.

---

[275] Minute Kyd to PS/SofS [MOD], 5 July 2007, 'CDS visit to Iraq 1-3 Jul 07'.
[276] Letter Shaw to Houghton, 14 August 2007, 'Post operation report Shawforce Jan-Aug 07'.
[277] JIC Assessment, 27 February 2008, 'Iraq: Security Prospects in the South'.

787. ACM Stirrup's conclusion that there was no need to review UK drawdown plans was premature in the light of both the level of uncertainty generated by the Charge of the Knights and continued questions about the ability of the ISF to take the security lead in Basra.

Did the UK achieve its objectives in Iraq?

788. From mid-2005 onwards, various senior individuals – officials, military officers and Ministers – began to consider whether the UK was heading towards "strategic failure" in Iraq.

789. The term "strategic failure" was variously used to mean:

- the development of a widespread sectarian conflict or civil war in Iraq;
- "victory" for terrorist groups;
- collapse of the democratic process;
- failure to achieve the UK's objectives;
- failure to achieve a stable and secure environment in Basra;
- the collapse of the UK/Iraq relationship;
- the division of Iraq and the end of its existence as a nation state;
- damage to the UK's military and political reputation; and
- damage to the relationship between the US and UK.

790. None of the contemporary accounts that the Inquiry has considered reached the conclusion that strategic failure was inevitable, although most recognised that without some form of corrective action it was a serious risk.

791. Although the UK revisited its Iraq strategy with considerable frequency, no substantial change in approach was ever implemented: UK troop numbers continued to reduce; the size of the civilian deployment varied very little; the Iraqiisation of security and handover of responsibility to the Iraqi Government remained key objectives.

792. The Iraq of 2009 certainly did not meet the UK's objectives as described in January 2003: it fell far short of strategic success. Although the borders of Iraq were the same as they had been in 2003, deep sectarian divisions threatened both stability and unity. Those divisions were not created by the coalition, but they were exacerbated by its decisions on de-Ba'athification and on demobilisation of the Iraqi Army and were not addressed by an effective programme of reconciliation.

793. In January 2009, the JIC judged "internal political failures that could lead to renewed violence within and between Iraq's Sunni, Shia and Kurdish communities"[278] to be the greatest strategic threat to Iraq's stability.

---

[278] JIC Assessment, 28 January 2009, 'Iraq: Threats to Stability and UK Mission Change in 2009'.

794. The fragility of the situation in Basra, which had been the focus of UK effort in MND(SE), was clear. The JIC assessed that threats remained from Iranian-backed JAM Special Groups, and the Iraqi Security Forces remained reliant on support from Multi-National Forces to address weaknesses in leadership and tactical support. Even as UK troops withdrew from Basra, the US was sufficiently concerned to deploy its own forces there, to secure the border and protect supply lines.

795. In 2009, Iraq did have a democratically elected Parliament, in which many of Iraq's communities were represented. But, as demonstrated by the protracted process of negotiating agreements on the status of US and then UK forces in Iraq, and the continued absence of a much-needed Hydrocarbons Law, representation did not translate into effective government. In 2008, Transparency International judged Iraq to be the third most corrupt country in the world, and in mid-2009 the Assessments Staff judged that Government ministries were "riddled with" corruption.[279]

796. By 2009, it had been demonstrated that some elements of the UK's 2003 objectives for Iraq were misjudged. No evidence had been identified that Iraq possessed weapons of mass destruction, with which it might threaten its neighbours and the international community more widely. But in the years between 2003 and 2009, events in Iraq had undermined regional stability, including by allowing Al Qaida space in which to operate and unsecured borders across which its members might move.

797. The gap between the ambitious objectives with which the UK entered Iraq and the resources that the Government was prepared to commit to the task was substantial from the start. Even with more resources it would have been difficult to achieve those objectives, as a result of the circumstances of the invasion, the lack of international support, the inadequacy of planning and preparation, and the inability to deliver law and order. The lack of security hampered progress at every turn. It is therefore not surprising that, despite the considerable efforts made by UK civilian and military personnel over this period, the results were meagre.

798. The Inquiry has not been able to identify alternative approaches that would have guaranteed greater success in the circumstances of March 2003. What can be said is that a number of opportunities for the sort of candid reappraisal of policies that would have better aligned objectives and resources did not take place. There was no serious consideration of more radical options, such as an early withdrawal or else a substantial increase in effort. The Inquiry has identified a number of moments, especially during the first year of the Occupation, when it would have been possible to conduct a substantial reappraisal. None took place.

---

[279] CIG Assessment, 21 July 2009, 'How Corrupt is Iraq?'

Key findings

Development of UK strategy and options, 9/11 to early January 2002

799. The following key findings are from Section 3.1:

- After the attacks on the US on 9/11, Mr Blair declared that the UK would stand "shoulder to shoulder" with the US to defeat and eradicate international terrorism.

- Mr Blair took an active and leading role throughout the autumn of 2001 in building a coalition to act against that threat, including taking military action against the Taliban regime in Afghanistan.

- Mr Blair also emphasised the potential risk of terrorists acquiring and using a nuclear, biological or chemical weapon, and the dangers of inaction.

- In relation to Iraq, Mr Blair sought to influence US policy and prevent precipitate military action by the US, which he considered would undermine the success of the coalition which had been established for action against international terrorism. He recommended identifying an alternative policy which would command widespread international support.

- In December 2001, Mr Blair suggested a strategy for regime change in Iraq that would build over time, including "if necessary" taking military action without losing international support.

- The tactics chosen by Mr Blair were to emphasise the threat which Iraq might pose, rather than a more balanced consideration of both Iraq's capabilities and intent; and to offer the UK's support for President Bush in an effort to influence his decisions on how to proceed.

- That remained Mr Blair's approach in the months that followed.

Development of UK strategy and options, January to April 2002 – "axis of evil" to Crawford

800. The following key findings are from Section 3.2:

- The UK continued to pursue implementation of the "smarter" economic sanctions regime in the first months of 2002, but continuing divisions between Permanent Members of the Security Council meant there was no agreement on the way forward.

- In public statements at the end of February and in the first week of March 2002, Mr Blair and Mr Straw set out the view that Iraq was a threat which had to be dealt with.

- At Cabinet on 7 March, Mr Blair and Mr Straw emphasised that no decisions had been taken and Cabinet was not being asked to take decisions. Cabinet endorsed the conclusion that Iraq's weapons of mass destruction (WMD) programmes posed a threat to peace and endorsed a strategy of engaging closely with the US Government in order to shape policy and its presentation.

- At Crawford, Mr Blair offered President Bush a partnership in dealing urgently with the threat posed by Saddam Hussein. He proposed that the UK and US should pursue a strategy based on an ultimatum calling on Iraq to permit the return of weapons inspectors or face the consequences.

- Following his meeting with President Bush, Mr Blair stated that Saddam Hussein had to be confronted and brought back into compliance with the UN.

- The acceptance of the possibility that the UK might participate in a military invasion of Iraq was a profound change in UK thinking. Although no decisions had been taken, that became the basis for contingency planning in the months ahead.

Development of UK strategy and options, April to July 2002

801. The following key findings are from Section 3.3:

- By July 2002, the UK Government had concluded that President Bush was impatient to move on Iraq and that the US might take military action in circumstances that would be difficult for the UK.

- Mr Blair's Note to President Bush of 28 July sought to persuade President Bush to use the UN to build a coalition for action by seeking a partnership with the US and setting out a framework for action.

- Mr Blair told President Bush that the UN was the simplest way to encapsulate a "casus belli" in some defining way, with an ultimatum to Iraq once military forces started to build up in October. That might be backed by a UN resolution.

- Mr Blair's Note, which had not been discussed or agreed with his colleagues, set the UK on a path leading to diplomatic activity in the UN and the possibility of participation in military action in a way that would make it very difficult for the UK subsequently to withdraw its support for the US.

Development of UK strategy and options, late July to 14 September 2002

802. The following key findings are from Section 3.4:

- In discussions with the US over the summer of 2002, Mr Blair and Mr Straw sought to persuade the US Administration to secure multilateral support before taking action on Iraq; and to do so through the UN. They proposed a strategy in which the first objective was to offer Iraq the opportunity and last chance to comply with its obligations to disarm.

- If Iraq did not take that opportunity and military action was required, the UK was seeking to establish conditions whereby such action would command multilateral support and be taken with the authority of the Security Council.

- Mr Blair also decided to publish an explanation of why action was needed to deal with Iraq; and to recall Parliament to debate the issue.

- The UK made a significant contribution to President Bush's decision, announced on 12 September, to take the issue of Iraq back to the UN.

- Statements made by China, France and Russia after President Bush's speech highlighted the different positions of the five Permanent Members of the Security Council, in particular about the role of the Council in deciding whether military action was justified. As a result, the negotiation of resolution 1441 was complex and difficult.

Development of UK strategy and options, September to November 2002 – the negotiation of resolution 1441

803. The following key findings are from Section 3.5:

- The declared objective of the US and UK was to obtain international support within the framework of the UN for a strategy of coercive diplomacy for the disarmament of Iraq. For the UK, regime change was a means to achieve disarmament, not an objective in its own right.

- The negotiation of resolution 1441 reflected a broad consensus in the UN Security Council on the need to achieve the disarmament of Iraq.

- To secure consensus in the Security Council despite the different positions of the US and France and Russia, resolution 1441 was a compromise containing drafting 'fixes'.

- That created deliberate ambiguities on a number of key issues including: the level of non-compliance with resolution 1441 which would constitute a material breach; by whom that determination would be made; and whether there would be a second resolution explicitly authorising the use of force.

Development of UK strategy and options, November 2002 to January 2003

804. The following key findings are from Section 3.6:

- Following the adoption of resolution 1441, the UK was pursuing a strategy of coercive diplomacy to secure the disarmament of Iraq. The hope was that this might be achieved by peaceful means, but views differed on how likely that would be.

- The UK Government remained convinced that Iraq had retained prohibited weapons and was pursuing chemical, biological and ballistic missile programmes in contravention of its obligations to disarm; and that the absence of evidence of weapons and programmes was the result of a successful policy of concealment.

- By early January 2003, Mr Blair had concluded that Iraq had had "no change of heart" and military action to remove Saddam Hussein's regime was likely to be required to disarm Iraq.

- The US Administration was planning military action no later than early March.

- Mr Blair and Mr Straw concluded that a second UN resolution would be essential to secure domestic and international support for military action. In the absence of a "smoking gun", that would require more time and a series of reports from the UN inspectors which established a pattern of Iraqi non-compliance with its obligations.

- Mr Blair secured President Bush's support for a second resolution but did not secure agreement that the inspections process should continue until the end of March or early April. That left little time for the inspections process to provide the evidence that would be needed to achieve international agreement on the way ahead.

Development of UK strategy and options, 1 February to 7 March 2003

805. The following key findings are from Section 3.7:

- By the time the Security Council met on 7 March 2003 there were deep divisions within it on the way ahead on Iraq.

- Following President Bush's agreement to support a second resolution to help Mr Blair, Mr Blair and Mr Straw continued during February and early March 2003 to develop the position that Saddam Hussein was not co-operating as required by resolution 1441 (2002) and, if that situation continued, a second resolution should be adopted stating that Iraq had failed to take the final opportunity offered by the Security Council.

- On 6 February, Mr Blair said that the UK would consider military action without a further resolution only if the inspectors reported that they could not do their job and a resolution was vetoed unreasonably. The UK would not take military action without a majority in the Security Council.

- Mr Blair's proposals, on 19 February, for a side statement defining tough tests for Iraq's co-operation and a deadline of 14 March for a vote by the Security Council, were not agreed by the US.

- The initial draft of a US, UK and Spanish resolution tabled on 24 February, which simply invited the Security Council to decide that Iraq had failed to take the final opportunity offered by resolution 1441, failed to attract support.

- Throughout February, the divisions in the Security Council widened.

- France, Germany and Russia set out their common position on 10 and 24 February. Their joint Memorandum of 24 February called for a programme of continued and reinforced inspections with a clear timeline and a military build-up to exert maximum pressure on Iraq to disarm.

- The reports to the Security Council by the IAEA reported increasing indications of Iraqi co-operation. On 7 March, Dr ElBaradei reported that there was no indication that Iraq had resumed nuclear activities and that it should be able to provide the Security Council with an assessment of Iraq's activities in the near future.

- Dr Blix reported to the Security Council on 7 March that there had been an acceleration of initiatives from Iraq and, while they did not constitute immediate co-operation, they were welcome. UNMOVIC would be proposing a work programme for the Security Council's approval, based on key tasks for Iraq to address. It would take months to verify sites and items, analyse documents, interview relevant personnel and draw conclusions.

- A revised draft US, UK and Spanish resolution, tabled after the reports by Dr Blix and Dr ElBaradei on 7 March and proposing a deadline of 17 March for Iraq to demonstrate full co-operation, also failed to attract support.

- China, France and Russia all stated that they did not favour a resolution authorising the use of force and that the Security Council should maintain its efforts to find a peaceful solution.

- Sir Jeremy Greenstock advised that a "side statement" with defined benchmarks for Iraqi co-operation could be needed to secure support from Mexico and Chile.

- Mr Blair told President Bush that he would need a majority of nine votes in the Security Council for Parliamentary approval for UK military action.

Iraq WMD assessments, pre-July 2002

806. The following key findings are from Section 4.1:

- The ingrained belief that Saddam Hussein's regime retained chemical and biological warfare capabilities, was determined to preserve and if possible enhance its capabilities, including at some point in the future a nuclear capability, and was pursuing an active policy of deception and concealment, had underpinned the UK Government's policy towards Iraq since the Gulf Conflict ended in 1991.

- Iraq's chemical, biological and ballistic missile programmes were seen as a threat to international peace and security in the Middle East, but overall, the threat from Iraq was viewed as less serious than that from other key countries of concern – Iran, Libya and North Korea.

- The Assessments issued by the Joint Intelligence Committee (JIC) reflected the uncertainties within the intelligence community about the detail of Iraq's activities.

- The statements prepared for, and used by, the UK Government in public from late 2001 onwards conveyed more certainty than the JIC Assessments about Iraq's proscribed activities and the potential threat they posed.

- The tendency to refer in public statements only to Iraq's "weapons of mass destruction" was likely to have created the impression that Iraq posed a greater threat than the detailed JIC Assessments would have supported.

- There was nothing in the JIC Assessments issued before July 2002 that would have raised any questions in policy-makers' minds about the core construct of Iraq's capabilities and intent. Indeed, from May 2001 onwards, the perception conveyed was that Iraqi activity could have increased since the departure of the weapons inspectors, funded by Iraq's growing illicit income from circumventing the sanctions regime.

- In the light of sensitivities about their content and significance, publication of documents on 'Iraq's Weapons of Mass Destruction', 'Weapons Inspections' and 'Abuse of Human Rights' was postponed until the policy on Iraq was clearer.

Iraq WMD assessments, July to September 2002

807. The following key findings are from Section 4.2:

- The urgency and certainty with which the Government stated that Iraq was a threat which had to be dealt with fuelled the demand for publication of the dossier and led to Mr Blair's decision to publish it in September, separate from any decision on the way ahead.

- The dossier was designed to "make the case" and secure Parliamentary and public support for the Government's position that action was urgently required to secure Iraq's disarmament.

- The JIC accepted ownership of the dossier and agreed its content. There is no evidence that intelligence was improperly included in the dossier or that No.10 improperly influenced the text.

- The assessed intelligence had not established beyond doubt either that Saddam Hussein had continued to produce chemical and biological weapons or that efforts to develop nuclear weapons continued. The JIC should have made that clear to Mr Blair.

- In his statement to Parliament on 24 September 2002, Mr Blair presented Iraq's past, current and potential future capabilities as evidence of the severity of the potential threat from Iraq's weapons of mass destruction; and that at some point in the future that threat would become a reality.

- The dossier's description of Iraq's capabilities and intent became part of the baseline against which the UK Government measured Iraq's future statements and actions and the success of weapons inspections.

- The widespread perception that the September 2002 dossier overstated the firmness of the evidence has produced a damaging legacy which may make it more difficult to secure support for Government policy, including military action, where the evidence depends on inferential judgements drawn from intelligence.

- There are lessons which should be implemented in using information from JIC Assessments to underpin policy decisions.

Iraq WMD assessments, October 2002 to March 2003

808. The following key findings are from Section 4.3:

- The ingrained belief already described in this Section underpinned the UK Government's position that Iraq was a threat that had to be dealt with and it needed to disarm or be disarmed. That remained the case up to and beyond the decision to invade Iraq in March 2003.

- The judgements about Iraq's capabilities and intentions relied too heavily on Iraq's past behaviour being a reliable indicator of its current and future actions.

- There was no consideration of whether, faced with the prospect of a US-led invasion, Saddam Hussein had taken a different position.

- The JIC made the judgements in the UK Government September dossier part of the test for Iraq.

- Iraq's statements that it had no weapons or programmes were dismissed as further evidence of a strategy of denial.

- The extent to which the JIC's judgements depended on inference and interpretation of Iraq's previous attitudes and behaviour was not recognised.

- At no stage was the hypothesis that Iraq might no longer have chemical, biological or nuclear weapons or programmes identified and examined by either the JIC or the policy community.

- A formal reassessment of the JIC's judgements should have taken place after Dr Blix's report to the Security Council on 14 February 2003 or, at the very latest, after his report of 7 March.

- Intelligence and assessments made by the JIC about Iraq's capabilities and intent continued to be used to prepare briefing material to support Government statements in a way which conveyed certainty without acknowledging the limitations of the intelligence.

- The independence and impartiality of the JIC remains of the utmost importance.

- SIS had a responsibility to ensure that key recipients of its reporting were informed in a timely way when doubts arose about key sources and when, subsequently, intelligence was withdrawn.

The search for WMD

809. The following key findings are from Section 4.4:

- The search for evidence of WMD in Iraq was started during the military campaign by Exploitation Task Force-75 and was carried forward from June 2003 by the Iraq Survey Group (ISG). The UK participated in both.

- As the insurgency developed, the ISG's operating conditions became increasingly difficult. There was competition for resources between counter-terrorism operations and the search for WMD evidence, and some ISG staff were diverted to the former.

- Mr Blair took a close interest in the work of the ISG and the presentation of its reports and the wider narrative about WMD. He raised the subject with President Bush.

- The Government was confident that pre-conflict assessments of Iraq's WMD capabilities would be confirmed once Saddam Hussein's regime had been removed.

- It quickly became apparent that it was unlikely that significant stockpiles would be found. This led to challenges to the credibility of both the Government and the intelligence community.

- There were soon demands for an independent judge-led inquiry into the pre-conflict intelligence.

- The Government was quick to acknowledge the need for a review, rejecting an independent inquiry in favour of reviews initiated by the House of Commons Foreign Affairs Committee and the Intelligence and Security Committee of Parliament.

- The Government's reluctance to establish an independent public inquiry became untenable in January 2004 when President Bush announced his own decision to set up an independent inquiry in the US.

- Faced with criticism of the pre-conflict intelligence and the absence of evidence of a current Iraqi WMD capability, Mr Blair sought to defend the decision to take military action by emphasising instead:
  - Saddam Hussein's strategic intent;
  - the regime's breaches of Security Council resolutions; and
  - the positive impact of military action in Iraq on global counter-proliferation efforts.

- The ISG's principal findings – that Iraq's WMD capability had mostly been destroyed in 1991 but that it had been Saddam Hussein's strategic intent to preserve the capability to reconstitute his WMD – were significant, but did not support statements made by the UK and US Governments before the invasion, which had focused on Iraq's current capabilities and an urgent and growing threat.

- The explanation for military action put forward by Mr Blair in October 2004 drew on the ISG's findings, but was not the explanation given before the conflict.

Advice on the legal basis for military action, November 2002 to March 2003

810. The following key findings are from Section 5:

- On 9 December, formal 'instructions' to provide advice were sent to Lord Goldsmith. They were sent by the FCO on behalf of the FCO and the MOD as well as No.10. The instructions made it clear that Lord Goldsmith should not provide an immediate response.

- Until 27 February, No.10 could not have been sure that Lord Goldsmith would advise that there was a basis on which military action against Iraq could be taken in the absence of a further decision of the Security Council.

- Lord Goldsmith's formal advice of 7 March set out alternative interpretations of the legal effect of resolution 1441. While Lord Goldsmith remained "of the opinion that the safest legal course would be to secure a second resolution", he concluded (paragraph 28) that "a reasonable case can be made that resolution 1441 was capable of reviving the authorisation in resolution 678 without a further resolution".

- Lord Goldsmith wrote that a reasonable case did not mean that if the matter ever came to court, he would be confident that the court would agree with this view. He judged a court might well conclude that OPs 4 and 12 required a further Security Council decision in order to revive the authorisation in resolution 678.

- At a meeting on 11 March, there was concern that the advice did not offer a clear indication that military action would be lawful. Lord Goldsmith was asked, after the meeting, by Admiral Boyce on behalf of the Armed Forces, and by the Treasury Solicitor, Ms Juliet Wheldon, in respect of the Civil Service, to give a clear-cut answer on whether military action would be lawful rather than unlawful.

- Lord Goldsmith concluded on 13 March that, on balance, the "better view" was that the conditions for the operation of the revival argument were met in this case, meaning that there was a lawful basis for the use of force without a further resolution beyond resolution 1441.

- Mr Brummell wrote to Mr Rycroft on 14 March:

  "It is an essential part of the legal basis for military action without a further resolution of the Security Council that there is strong evidence that Iraq has failed to comply with and co-operate fully in the implementation of resolution 1441 and has thus failed to take the final opportunity offered by the Security Council in that resolution. The Attorney General understands that it is unequivocally the Prime Minister's view that Iraq has committed further material breaches as specified in [operative] paragraph 4 of resolution 1441, but as this is a judgment for the Prime Minister, the Attorney would be grateful for confirmation that this is the case."

- Mr Rycroft replied to Mr Brummell on 15 March:

  "This is to confirm that it is indeed the Prime Minister's unequivocal view that Iraq is in further material breach of its obligations, as in OP4 [operative paragraph 4] of UNSCR 1441, because of 'false statements or omissions in the declarations submitted by Iraq pursuant to this resolution and failure to comply with, and co-operate fully in the interpretation of, this resolution'."

- Senior Ministers should have considered the question posed in Mr Brummell's letter of 14 March, either in the Defence and Overseas Policy Committee or a "War Cabinet", on the basis of formal advice. Such a Committee should then have reported its conclusions to Cabinet before its Members were asked to endorse the Government's policy.

- Cabinet was provided with the text of Lord Goldsmith's Written Answer to Baroness Ramsey setting out the legal basis for military action.

- That document represented a statement of the Government's legal position – it did not explain the legal basis of the conclusion that Iraq had failed to take "the final opportunity" to comply with its disarmament obligations offered by resolution 1441.

- Cabinet was not provided with written advice which set out, as the advice of 7 March had done, the conflicting arguments regarding the legal effect of resolution 1441 and whether, in particular, it authorised military action without a further resolution of the Security Council.

- The advice should have been provided to Ministers and senior officials whose responsibilities were directly engaged and should have been made available to Cabinet.

Development of the military options for an invasion of Iraq

811. The following key findings are from Section 6.1:

- The size and composition of a UK military contribution to the US-led invasion of Iraq was largely discretionary. The US wanted some UK capabilities (including Special Forces), to use UK bases, and the involvement of the UK military to avoid the perception of unilateral US military action. The primary impetus to maximise the size of the UK contribution and the recommendations on its composition came from the Armed Forces, with the agreement of Mr Hoon.

- From late February 2002, the UK judged that Saddam Hussein's regime could only be removed by a US-led invasion.

- In April 2002, the MOD advised that, if the US mounted a major military operation, the UK should contribute a division comprising three brigades. That was perceived to be commensurate with the UK's capabilities and the demands of the campaign. Anything smaller risked being compared adversely to the UK's contribution to the liberation of Kuwait in 1991.

- The MOD saw a significant military contribution as a means of influencing US decisions.

- Mr Blair and Mr Hoon wanted to keep open the option of contributing significant forces for ground operations as long as possible, but between May and mid-October consistently pushed back against US assumptions that the UK would provide a division.

- Air and maritime forces were offered to the US for planning purposes in September.

- The MOD advised in October that the UK was at risk of being excluded from US plans unless it offered ground forces, "Package 3", on the same basis as air and maritime forces. That could also significantly reduce the UK's vulnerability to US requests to provide a substantial and costly contribution to post-conflict operations.

- From August until December 2002, other commitments meant that UK planning for Package 3 was based on providing a divisional headquarters and an armoured brigade for operations in northern Iraq. That was seen as the maximum practicable contribution the UK could generate within the predicted timescales for US action.

- The deployment was dependent on Turkey's agreement to the transit of UK forces.

- Mr Blair agreed to offer Package 3 on 31 October 2002.

- That decision and its potential consequences were not formally considered by a Cabinet Committee or reported to Cabinet.

- In December 2002, the deployment of 3 Commando Brigade was identified as a way for the UK to make a valuable contribution in the initial stages of a land campaign if transit through Turkey was refused. The operational risks were not explicitly addressed.

- Following a visit to Turkey on 7 to 8 January 2003, Mr Hoon concluded that there would be no agreement to the deployment of UK ground forces through Turkey.

- By that time, in any case, the US had asked the UK to deploy for operations in southern Iraq.

Military planning for the invasion, January to March 2003

812. The following key findings are from Section 6.2:

- The decisions taken between mid-December 2002 and mid-January 2003 to increase the combat force deployed to three brigades and bring forward the date on which UK forces might participate in combat operations compressed the timescales available for preparation.

- The decision to deploy a large scale force for potential combat operations was taken without collective Ministerial consideration of the decision and its implications.

- The large scale force deployed was a one-shot capability. It would have been difficult to sustain the force if combat operations had been delayed until autumn 2003 or longer, and it constrained the capabilities which were available for a UK military contribution to post-conflict operations.

Military equipment (pre-conflict)

813. The following key findings are from Section 6.3:

- The decisions taken between mid-December 2002 and mid-January 2003 to increase combat forces and bring forward the date on which UK forces might participate in combat operations compressed the timescales available for preparation.

- The achievements made in preparing the forces in the time available were very considerable, but the deployment of forces more quickly than anticipated in the Defence Planning Assumptions meant that there were some serious equipment shortfalls when conflict began.

- Those shortfalls were exacerbated by the lack of an effective asset tracking system, a lesson from previous operations and exercises that the MOD had identified but not adequately addressed.

- Ministers were not fully aware of the risks inherent in the decisions and the MOD and PJHQ were not fully aware of the situation on the ground during the conflict.

Planning for a post-Saddam Hussein Iraq

814. The following key findings are from Section 6.4, and relate to evidence in Sections 6.4 and 6.5:

- Before the invasion of Iraq, Ministers, senior officials and the UK military recognised that post-conflict civilian and military operations were likely to be the strategically decisive phase of the Coalition's engagement in Iraq.

- UK planning and preparation for the post-conflict phase of operations, which rested on the assumption that the UK would be able quickly to reduce its military presence in Iraq and deploy only a minimal number of civilians, were wholly inadequate.

- The information available to the Government before the invasion provided a clear indication of the potential scale of the post-conflict task and the significant risks associated with the UK's proposed approach.

- Foreseeable risks included post-conflict political disintegration and extremist violence in Iraq, the inadequacy of US plans, the UK's inability to exert significant influence on US planning and, in the absence of UN authorisation for the administration and reconstruction of post-conflict Iraq, the reluctance of potential international partners to contribute to the post-conflict effort.

- The Government, which lacked both clear Ministerial oversight of post-conflict strategy, planning and preparation, and effective co-ordination between government departments, failed to analyse or manage those risks adequately.

- Mr Blair, who recognised the significance of the post-conflict phase, did not press President Bush for definite assurances about US plans, did not consider or seek advice on whether the absence of a satisfactory plan called for reassessment of the terms of the UK's engagement and did not make agreement on such a plan a condition of UK participation in military action.

The invasion

815. The following key findings are from Section 8:

- It took less than a month to achieve the departure of Saddam Hussein and the fall of Baghdad.

- The decision to advance into Basra was made by military commanders on the ground.

- The UK was unprepared for the media response to the initial difficulties. It had also underestimated the need for sustained communication of key strategic messages to inform public opinion about the objectives and progress of the military campaign, including in Iraq.

- For any future military operations, arrangements to agree and disseminate key strategic messages need to be put in place, in both London and on the ground, before operations begin.

- The UK acceded to the post-invasion US request that it assume leadership of a military Area of Responsibility (AOR) encompassing four provinces in southern Iraq, a position it then held for six years, without a formal Ministerial decision and without carrying out a robust analysis of the strategic implications for the UK or the military's capacity to support the UK's potential obligations in the region.

The post-conflict period

816. The following key findings are from Section 9.8, and relate to evidence in Sections 9.1 to 9.7:

- Between 2003 and 2009, the UK's most consistent strategic objective in relation to Iraq was to reduce the level of its deployed forces.

- The UK struggled from the start to have a decisive effect on the Coalition Provisional Authority's (CPA's) policies, even though it was fully implicated in its decisions as joint Occupying Power.

- US and UK strategies for Iraq began to diverge almost immediately after the conflict. Although the differences were managed, by early 2007 the UK was finding it difficult to play down the divergence, which was, by that point, striking.

- The UK missed clear opportunities to reconsider its military approach in Multi-National Division (South-East).

- Throughout 2004 and 2005, it appears that senior members of the Armed Forces reached the view that little more would be achieved in MND(SE) and that it would make more sense to concentrate military effort on Afghanistan where it might have greater effect.

- From July 2005 onwards, decisions in relation to resources for Iraq were made under the influence of the demands of the UK effort in Afghanistan. Although Iraq remained the stated UK main effort, the Government no longer had the option of a substantial reinforcement of its forces there.

- The UK's plans to reduce troop levels depended on the transition of lead responsibility for security to the Iraqi Security Forces, even as the latter's ability to take on that responsibility was in question.

- The UK spent time and energy on rewriting strategies, which tended to describe a desired end state without setting out how it would be reached.

- UK forces withdrew from Iraq in 2009 in circumstances which did not meet objectives defined in January 2003.

Reconstruction

817. The following key findings are from Section 10.4, and relate to evidence in Sections 10.1 to 10.3:

- The UK failed to plan or prepare for the major reconstruction programme required in Iraq.

- Reconstruction was the third pillar in a succession of UK strategies for Iraq. The Government never resolved how reconstruction would support broader UK objectives.

- Following the resignation of Ms Clare Short, the International Development Secretary, and the adoption of UN Security Council resolution 1483 in May 2003, DFID assumed leadership of the UK's reconstruction effort in Iraq. DFID would subsequently define, within the framework established by the Government, the scope and nature of that effort.

- At key points, DFID should have considered strategic questions about the scale, focus and purpose of the UK's reconstruction effort in Iraq.

- The US-led Coalition Provisional Authority excluded the UK from discussions on oil policy and on disbursements from the Development Fund for Iraq.

- Many of the failures which affected pre-invasion planning and preparation persisted throughout the post-conflict period. They included poor inter-departmental co-ordination, inadequate civilian military co-operation and a failure to use resources coherently.

- An unstable and insecure environment made it increasingly difficult to make progress on reconstruction. Although staff and contractors developed innovative ways to deliver projects and manage risks, the constraints were never overcome. Witnesses to the Inquiry identified some successes, in particular in building the capacity of central Iraqi Government institutions and the provincial government in Basra.

- Lessons learned through successive reviews of the UK approach to post-conflict reconstruction and stabilisation, in Iraq and elsewhere, were not applied in Iraq.

De-Ba'athification

818. The following key findings are from Section 11.2, and relate to evidence in Section 11.1:

- Early decisions on the form of de-Ba'athification and its implementation had a significant and lasting negative impact on Iraq.

- Limiting de-Ba'athification to the top three tiers of the party, rather than extending it to the fourth, would have had the potential to be far less damaging to Iraq's post-invasion recovery and political stability.

- The UK's ability to influence the CPA decision on the scope of the policy was limited and informal.

- The UK chose not to act on its well-founded misgivings about handing over the implementation of de-Ba'athification policy to the Governing Council.

Security Sector Reform

819. The following key findings are from Section 12.2, and relate to evidence in Section 12.1:

- Between 2003 and 2009, there was no coherent US/UK strategy for Security Sector Reform (SSR).

- The UK began work on SSR in Iraq without a proper understanding of what it entailed and hugely underestimated the magnitude of the task.

- The UK was unable to influence the US or engage it in a way that produced an Iraq-wide approach.

- There was no qualitative way for the UK to measure progress. The focus on the quantity of officers trained for the Iraqi Security Forces, rather than the quality of officers, was simplistic and gave a misleading sense of comfort.

- After 2006, the UK's determination to withdraw from Iraq meant that aspirations for the Iraqi Security Forces were lowered to what would be "good enough" for Iraq. It was never clear what that meant in practice.

- The development of the Iraqi Army was considerably more successful than that of the Iraqi Police Service. But the UK was still aware before it withdrew from Iraq that the Iraqi Army had not been sufficiently tested. The UK was not confident that the Iraqi Army could maintain security without support.

Resources

820. The following key findings are from Section 13.2, and relate to evidence in Section 13.1:

- The direct cost of the conflict in Iraq was at least £9.2bn (the equivalent of £11.83bn in 2016). In total, 89 percent of that was spent on military operations.

- The Government's decision to take part in military action against Iraq was not affected by consideration of the potential financial cost to the UK of the invasion or the post-conflict period.

- Ministers were not provided with estimates of military conflict and post-conflict costs, or with advice on their affordability, when decisions were taken on the scale of the UK's military contribution to a US-led invasion of Iraq, and on the UK's role in the post-conflict period. They should have been.

- There was no articulated need for additional financial resources for military operations in Iraq that was not met.

- The arrangements for funding military Urgent Operational Requirements and other military costs worked as intended, and did not constrain the UK military's ability to conduct operations in Iraq.

- The controls imposed by the Treasury on the MOD's budget in September 2003 did not constrain the UK military's ability to conduct operations in Iraq.

- The Government was slow to recognise that Iraq was an enduring operation, and to adapt its funding arrangements to support both military operations and civilian activities.

- The arrangements for securing funding for civilian activities could be slow and unpredictable. Some high-priority civilian activities were funded late or only in part.

Military equipment (post-conflict)

821. The following key findings are from Section 14.2, and relate to evidence in Section 14.1:

- Between 2003 and 2009, UK forces in Iraq faced gaps in some key capability areas, including protected mobility, Intelligence, Surveillance, Target Acquisition and Reconnaissance (ISTAR) and helicopter support.

- It was not sufficiently clear which person or department within the MOD had responsibility for identifying and articulating capability gaps.

- Delays in providing adequate medium weight Protected Patrol Vehicles (PPVs) and the failure to meet the needs of UK forces in MND(SE) for ISTAR and helicopters should not have been tolerated.

- The MOD was slow in responding to the developing threat in Iraq from Improvised Explosive Devices (IEDs). The range of protected mobility options available to commanders in MND(SE) was limited. Although work had begun before 2002 to source an additional PPV, it was only ordered in July 2006 following Ministerial intervention.

- Funding was not a direct barrier to the identification and deployment of additional solutions to the medium weight PPV gap. But it appears that the longer-term focus of the Executive Committee of the Army Board on the Future Rapid Effect System programme inhibited it from addressing the more immediate issue related to medium weight PPV capability.

- The decision to deploy troops to Afghanistan had a material impact on the availability of key capabilities for deployment to Iraq, particularly helicopters and ISTAR.

Civilian personnel

822. The following key findings are from Section 15.2, and relate to evidence in Section 15.1:

- Before the invasion of Iraq, the Government had made only minimal preparations for the deployment of civilian personnel.

- There was an enduring gap between the Government's civilian capacity and the level of its ambition in Iraq.

- There was no overarching consideration by the Government of the extent to which civilians could be effective in a highly insecure environment, or of the security assets needed for civilians to do their jobs effectively.

- The evidence seen by the Inquiry indicates that the Government recognised its duty of care to UK-based and locally engaged civilians in Iraq. A significant effort was made to keep civilians safe in a dangerous environment.

Service Personnel

823. The following key findings are from Section 16.4, and relate to evidence in Sections 16.1 to 16.3:

- In 2002, the UK military was already operating at, and in some cases beyond, the limits of the guidelines agreed in the 1998 *Strategic Defence Review*. As a result, the Harmony Guidelines were being breached for some units and specialist trades.

- The Government's decision to contribute a military force to a US-led invasion of Iraq inevitably increased the risk that more Service Personnel would be put in breach of the Harmony Guidelines. The issue of the potential pressure on Service Personnel was not a consideration in the decision.

- The MOD planned and prepared effectively to provide medical care in support of Operation TELIC.

- There were major improvements in the provision of medical care, mental healthcare and rehabilitative care available to Service Personnel over the course of Op TELIC.

- Most of the contacts between the MOD and bereaved families were conducted with sensitivity. In a few cases, they were not. The MOD progressively improved how it engaged with and supported bereaved families, in part driven by consistent public and Ministerial pressure.

- The Government's decision in 2006 to deploy a second medium scale force to Helmand province in Afghanistan further increased the pressure on Service Personnel, on elements of the MOD's welfare, medical and investigative systems, and the coronial system.

- Much of the MOD's and the Government's effort from 2006 was focused on addressing those pressures.

- The MOD should have planned and prepared to address those pressures, rather than react to them.

- The Government should have acted sooner to address the backlog of inquests into the deaths of Service Personnel. The support it did provide, in June 2006, cleared the backlog.

- The MOD made a number of improvements to the Board of Inquiry process, but some proposals for more substantive reform (including the introduction of an independent member) were not fully explored. The MOD significantly improved the way it communicated with and supported bereaved families in relation to military investigations and inquests.

- The MOD was less effective at providing support to Service Personnel who were mobilised individually (a category which included almost all Reservists) and their families, than to formed units.

Civilian casualties

824. The following key findings are from Section 17:

- The Inquiry considers that a Government has a responsibility to make every reasonable effort to understand the likely and actual effects of its military actions on civilians.

- In the months before the invasion, Mr Blair emphasised the need to minimise the number of civilian casualties arising from an invasion of Iraq. The MOD's responses offered reassurance based on the tight targeting procedures governing the air campaign.

- The MOD made only a broad estimate of direct civilian casualties arising from an attack on Iraq, based on previous operations.

- With hindsight, greater efforts should have been made in the post-conflict period to determine the number of civilian casualties and the broader effects of military operations on civilians. More time was devoted to the question of which department should have responsibility for the issue of civilian casualties than it was to efforts to determine the actual number.

- The Government's consideration of the issue of Iraqi civilian casualties was driven by its concern to rebut accusations that Coalition Forces were responsible for the deaths of large numbers of civilians, and to sustain domestic support for operations in Iraq.

Lessons

825. In a number of Sections of this Report, the Inquiry has set out explicit lessons. They relate in particular to those elements of the UK's engagement in Iraq which might be replicated in future operations.

826. The decision to join the US-led invasion of Iraq in 2003 was the product of a particular set of circumstances which are unlikely to be repeated. Unlike other instances in which military force has been used, the invasion was not prompted by the aggression of another country or an unfolding humanitarian disaster. The lessons drawn by the Inquiry on the pre-conflict element of this Report are therefore largely context-specific and embedded in its conclusions. Lessons on collective Ministerial decision-making, where the principles identified are enduring ones, are an exception. They, and other lessons which have general application, are set out below.

The decision to go to war

827. In a democratic system, public support and understanding for a major military operation are essential. It is therefore important to guard against overstating what military action might achieve and against any tendency to play down the risks. A realistic assessment of the possibilities and limitations of armed force, and of the challenges of intervening in the affairs of other States, should help any future UK Government manage expectations, including its own.

828. When the potential for military action arises, the Government should not commit to a firm political objective before it is clear that it can be achieved. Regular reassessment is essential, to ensure that the assumptions upon which policy is being made and implemented remain correct.

829. Once an issue becomes a matter for the Security Council, the UK Government cannot expect to retain control of how it is to be discussed and eventually decided unless it is able to work with the interests and agendas of other Member States. In relation to Iraq, the independent role of the inspectors was a further dimension.

830. A military timetable should not be allowed to dictate a diplomatic timetable. If a strategy of coercive diplomacy is being pursued, forces should be deployed in such a way that the threat of action can be increased or decreased according to the diplomatic situation and the policy can be sustained for as long as necessary.

831. The issue of influencing the US, both at the strategic and at the operational level, was a constant preoccupation at all levels of the UK Government.

832. Prime Ministers will always wish to exercise their own political judgement on how to handle the relationship with the US. It will depend on personal relationships as well as on the nature of the issues being addressed. On all these matters of strategy and diplomacy, the Inquiry recognises that there is no standard formula that will be appropriate in all cases.

833. Whether or not influence has been exercised can be difficult to ascertain, even in retrospect. The views of allies are most likely to make a difference when they come in one side of an internal debate, and there are a number of instances where the UK arguments did make a difference to the formation and implementation of US policy. The US and UK are close allies, but the relationship between the two is unequal.

834. The exercise of influence will always involve a combination of identifying the prerequisites for success in a shared endeavour, and a degree of bargaining to make sure that the approach meets the national interest. In situations like the run-up to the invasion of Iraq:

- If certain measures are identified as prerequisite for success then their importance should be underlined from the start. There are no prizes for sharing a failure.

- Those measures that are most important should be pursued persistently and consistently.

- If it is assumed that a consequence of making a contribution in one area is that a further contribution would not be required in another, then that should be made explicit.

- Influence should not be set as an objective in itself. The exercise of influence is a means to an end.

Weapons of mass destruction

835. There will continue to be demands for factual evidence to explain the background to controversial policy decisions including, where appropriate, the explicit and public use of assessed intelligence.

836. The Inquiry shares the Butler Review's conclusions that it was a mistake not to see the risk of combining in the September dossier the JIC's assessment of intelligence and other evidence with the interpretation and presentation of the evidence in order to make the case for policy action.

837. The nature of the two functions is fundamentally different. As can be seen from the JIC Assessments quoted in, and published with, this report, they contain careful language intended to ensure that no more weight is put on the evidence than it can bear. Organising the evidence in order to present an argument in the language of Ministerial statements produces a quite different type of document.

838. The widespread perception that the September 2002 dossier overstated the firmness of the evidence about Iraq's capabilities and intentions in order to influence opinion and "make the case" for action to disarm Iraq has produced a damaging legacy, including undermining trust and confidence in Government statements, particularly those which rely on intelligence which cannot be independently verified.

839. As a result, in situations where the policy response may involve military action and the evidence, at least in part, depends on inferential judgements drawn from necessarily incomplete intelligence, it may be more difficult to secure support for the Government's position and agreement to action.

840. The explicit and public use of material from JIC Assessments to underpin policy decisions will be infrequent. But, from the evidence on the compilation of the September dossier, the lessons for any similar exercise in future would be:

- The need for clear separation of the responsibility for analysis and assessment of intelligence from the responsibility for making the argument for a policy.

- The importance of precision in describing the position. In the case of the September dossier, for instance, the term "programme" was used to describe disparate activities at very different stages of maturity. There was a "programme" to extend the range of the Al Samoud missile. There was no "programme" in any meaningful sense to develop and produce nuclear weapons. Use of the shorthand CW or BW in relation to Iraq's capability obscured whether the reference was to weapons or warfare. Constant use of the term "weapons of mass destruction" without further clarification obscured the differences between the potential impact of nuclear, biological and chemical weapons and the ability to deliver them effectively. For example, there would be a considerable difference between the effects of an artillery shell filled with mustard gas, which is a battlefield weapon, and a long-range ballistic missile with a chemical or biological warhead, which is a weapon of terror.

- The need to identify and accurately describe the confidence and robustness of the evidence base. There may be evidence which is "authoritative" or which puts an issue "beyond doubt"; but there are unlikely to be many circumstances when those descriptions could properly be applied to inferential judgements relying on intelligence.

- The need to be explicit about the likelihood of events. The possibility of Iraq producing and using an improvised nuclear device was, rightly, omitted from the dossier. But the claim that Iraq could build a nuclear weapon within one to two years if it obtained fissile material <u>and</u> other essential components from foreign sources was included without addressing how feasible and likely that would be. In addition, the Executive Summary gave prominence to the International Institute of Strategic Studies suggestion that Iraq would be able to assemble nuclear weapons within months if it could obtain fissile material, without reference to the material in the main text of the dossier which made clear that the UK took a very different view.

- The need to be scrupulous in discriminating between facts and knowledge on the one hand and opinion, judgement or belief on the other.

- The need for vigilance to avoid unwittingly crossing the line from supposition to certainty, including by constant repetition of received wisdom.

841. When assessed intelligence is explicitly and publicly used to support a policy decision, there would be benefit in subjecting that assessment and the underpinning intelligence to subsequent scrutiny, by a suitable, independent body, such as the Intelligence and Security Committee, with a view to identifying lessons for the future.

842. In the context of the lessons from the preparation of the September 2002 dossier, the Inquiry identifies in Section 4.2 the benefits of separating the responsibilities for assessment of intelligence from setting out the arguments in support of a policy.

843. The evidence in Section 4.3 reinforces that lesson. It shows that the intelligence and assessments made by the JIC about Iraq's capabilities and intent continued to be used to prepare briefing material to support Government statements in a way which conveyed certainty without acknowledging the limitations of the intelligence.

844. The independence and impartiality of the JIC remains of the utmost importance.

845. As the Foreign Affairs Committee report in July 2003 pointed out, the late Sir Percy Cradock wrote in his history of the JIC that:

"Ideally, intelligence and policy should be close but distinct. Too distinct and assessments become an in-growing, self-regarding activity, producing little or no work of interest to the decision-makers ... Too close a link and policy begins to play back on estimates, producing the answers the policy makers would like ... The analysts become courtiers, whereas their proper function is to report their findings ... without fear or favour. The best arrangement is intelligence and policy in separate but adjoining rooms, with communicating doors and thin partition walls ..."[280]

846. Mr Straw told the FAC in 2003:

"The reason why we have a Joint Intelligence Committee which is separate from the intelligence agencies is precisely so that those who are obtaining the intelligence are

---

[280] Cradock, Sir Percy. *Know your enemy – How the Joint Intelligence Committee saw the World*. John Murray, 2002.

not then directly making the assessment upon it. That is one of the very important strengths of our system compared with most other systems around the world."[281]

847. The FAC endorsed those sentiments.[282] It stated that the JIC has a "vital role in safeguarding the independence and impartiality of intelligence"; and that the "independence and impartiality of its own role" was "of the utmost importance". It recommended that Ministers should "bear in mind at all times the importance of ensuring that the JIC is free of all political pressure".

848. In its response to the FAC, the Government stated:

"We agree. The JIC plays a crucial role in providing the Government with objective assessments on a range of issues of importance to national interests."[283]

The invasion of Iraq

849. The military plan for the invasion of Iraq depended for success on a rapid advance on Baghdad, including convincing the Iraqi population of the Coalition's determination to remove the regime.

850. By the end of March, the Government had recognised the need for sustained communication of key strategic messages and improved capabilities to reach a range of audiences in the UK, Iraq and the wider international community. But there was clearly a need for more robust arrangements to integrate Coalition efforts in the UK, US and the forces deployed in Iraq.

851. The reaction of the media and the Iraqi population to perceived difficulties encountered within days of the start of an operation, which was planned to last up to 125 days, might have been anticipated if there had been more rigorous examination of possible scenarios pre-conflict and the media had better understood the original concept of operations and the nature of the Coalition responses to the situations they encountered once the campaign began.

852. The difficulty and complexity of successfully delivering distinct strategic messages to each of the audiences a government needs to reach should not be underestimated. For any future military operations, arrangements tailored to meet the circumstances of each operation need to be put in place in both London and on the ground before operations begin.

---

[281] Ninth Report from the Foreign Affairs Committee, Session 2002-2003, 7 July 2003, *The Decision to go to War in Iraq,* HC 813-1, paragraph 153.
[282] Ninth Report from the Foreign Affairs Committee, Session 2002-2003, 7 July 2003, *The Decision to go to War in Iraq,* HC 813-1, paragraphs 156-157.
[283] Foreign Secretary, November 2003, *The Decision to go to War in Iraq Response of the Secretary of State for Foreign and Commonwealth Affairs,* November 2003, Cm6062, paragraph 27.

853. When the UK acceded to the US request that it assume leadership of a military Area of Responsibility encompassing four provinces in southern Iraq, it did so without a robust analysis either of the strategic implications for the UK or of the military's capacity to support the UK's potential obligations in the region.

854. A step of such magnitude should be taken deliberately and having considered the wider strategic and resource implications and contingent liabilities.

855. That requires all government departments whose responsibilities will be engaged to have been formally involved in providing Ministers with coherent inter-departmental advice before decisions are taken; the proper function of the Cabinet Committee system.

The post-conflict period

856. The UK had not participated in an opposed invasion and full-scale occupation of a sovereign State (followed by shared responsibility for security and reconstruction over a long period) since the end of the Second World War. The particular circumstances of Op TELIC are unlikely to recur. Nevertheless, there are lessons to be drawn about major operations abroad and the UK's approach to armed intervention.

857. The UK did not achieve its objectives, despite the best efforts and acceptance of risk in a dangerous environment by military and civilian personnel.

858. Although the UK expected to be involved in Iraq for a lengthy period after the conflict, the Government was unprepared for the role in which the UK found itself from April 2003. Much of what went wrong stemmed from that lack of preparation.

859. In any undertaking of this kind, certain fundamental elements are of vital importance:

- the best possible appreciation of the theatre of operations, including the political, cultural and ethnic background, and the state of society, the economy and infrastructure;
- a hard-headed assessment of risks;
- objectives which are realistic within that context, and if necessary limited – rather than idealistic and based on optimistic assumptions; and
- allocation of the resources necessary for the task – both military and civil.

860. All of these elements were lacking in the UK's approach to its role in post-conflict Iraq.

861. Where responsibility is to be shared, it is essential to have written agreement in advance on how decision-making and governance will operate within an alliance or coalition. The UK normally acts with allies, as it did in Iraq. Within the NATO Alliance, the rules and mechanisms for decision-taking and the sharing of responsibility have been developed over time and are well understood. The Coalition in Iraq, by contrast, was an ad hoc alliance. The UK tried to establish some governance principles in the Memorandum of Understanding proposed to the US, but did not press the point. This led the UK into the uncomfortable and unsatisfactory situation of accepting shared responsibility without the ability to make a formal input to the process of decision-making.

862. As Iraq showed, the pattern set in the initial stage of an intervention is crucial. The maximum impact needs to be made in the early weeks and months, or opportunities missed may be lost for ever. It is very difficult to recover from a slow or damaging start.

863. Ground truth is vital. Over-optimistic assessments lead to bad decisions. Senior decision-makers – Ministers, Chiefs of Staff, senior officials – must have a flow of accurate and frank reporting. A "can do" attitude is laudably ingrained in the UK Armed Forces – a determination to get on with the job, however difficult the circumstances – but this can prevent ground truth from reaching senior ears. At times in Iraq, the bearers of bad tidings were not heard. On several occasions, decision-makers visiting Iraq (including the Prime Minister, the Foreign Secretary and the Chief of the General Staff) found the situation on the ground to be much worse than had been reported to them. Effective audit mechanisms need to be used to counter optimism bias, whether through changes in the culture of reporting, use of multiple channels of information – internal and external – or use of visits.

864. It is important to retain a flexible margin of resources – in personnel, equipment and financing – and the ability to change tactics to deal with adverse developments on the ground. In Iraq, that flexibility was lost after the parallel deployment to Helmand province in Afghanistan, which both constrained the supply of equipment (such as ISTAR) and took away the option of an effective reinforcement. Any decision to deploy to the limit of capabilities entails a high level of risk. In relation to Iraq, the risks involved in the parallel deployment of two enduring medium scale operations were not examined with sufficient rigour and challenge.

865. The management, in Whitehall, of a cross-government effort on the scale which was required in Iraq is a complex task. It needs dedicated leadership by someone with time, energy and influence. It cannot realistically be done by a Prime Minister alone, but requires a senior Minister with lead responsibility who has access to the Prime Minister and is therefore able to call on his or her influence in resolving problems or conflicts. A coherent inter-departmental effort, supported by a structure able to hold departments to account, is required to support such a Minister.

Reconstruction

866. The starting point for all discussions of reconstruction in circumstances comparable to those in Iraq between 2003 and 2009 must be that this is an area where progress will be extremely difficult.

867. Better planning and preparation for a post-Saddam Hussein Iraq would not necessarily have prevented the events that unfolded in Iraq between 2003 and 2009. It would not have been possible for the UK to prepare for every eventuality. Better plans and preparation could have mitigated some of the risks to which the UK and Iraq were exposed between 2003 and 2009 and increased the likelihood of achieving the outcomes desired by the UK and the Iraqi people.

868. From late 2003, successive reviews of the UK's approach to post-conflict reconstruction, later expanded to include the broader concept of stabilisation, resulted in a series of changes to the UK's approach to post-conflict operations. Despite those changes, many of the shortcomings that characterised the UK Government's approach to pre-conflict planning and preparation in 2002 and early 2003 persisted after the invasion.

869. The UK Government's new strategic framework for stabilisation, the new machinery for inter-departmental co-ordination and the enhanced resources now available for stabilisation operations continue to evolve. If future changes are to increase the effectiveness of UK operations, they must address the lessons for planning, preparation and implementation derived from the Iraq experience.

870. The lessons identified by the Inquiry apply to both the planning and preparation for post-conflict operations, of which reconstruction is a major but not the sole component, and to post-conflict operations themselves.

871. Analysis of the available material must draw on multiple perspectives, reflect dissenting views, identify risk – including that associated with any gaps in knowledge – and consider a range of options.

872. Information must be shared as widely across departments as is necessary to support that approach.

873. Gathering information and analysis of the nature and scale of the potential task should be systematic and as thorough as possible, and should capture the views and aspirations of local communities.

874. Plans derived from that analysis should:

- incorporate a range of options appropriate to different contingencies;
- reflect a realistic assessment of UK (and partners') resources and capabilities;
- integrate civilian and military objectives and capabilities in support of a single UK strategy;
- be exposed to scrutiny and challenge at Ministerial, senior official and expert level;
- be reviewed regularly and, if the strategic context, risk profile or projected cost changes significantly, be revised.

875. A government must prepare for a range of scenarios, not just the best case, and should not assume that it will be able to improvise.

876. Where the UK is the junior partner and is unable during planning or implementation to secure the outcome it requires, it should take stock of whether to attach conditions to continued participation and whether further involvement would be consistent with the UK's strategic interest.

877. Public statements on the extent of the UK's ambition should reflect a realistic assessment of what is achievable. To do otherwise is to risk even greater disillusionment and a loss of UK credibility.

878. Departmental priorities and interests will inevitably continue to diverge even where an inter-departmental body with a cross-government role, currently the Stabilisation Unit (SU), is in place. Therefore, co-operation between departments needs continual reinforcement at official and Ministerial levels.

879. The Head of the SU must be sufficiently senior and the SU enjoy recognition inside and outside government as a centre of excellence in its field if the Unit is to have credibility and influence in No.10, the National Security Council, the Treasury, the FCO, DFID and the MOD, and with the military.

De-Ba'athification

880. After the fall of a repressive regime, steps inevitably have to be taken to prevent those closely identified with that regime from continuing to hold positions of influence in public life. The development of plans which minimise undesired consequences, which are administered with justice and which are based on a robust understanding of the social context in which they will be implemented, should be an essential part of preparation for any post-conflict phase. This should include measures designed to address concerns within the wider population, including those of the victims of the old regime, and to promote reconciliation.

881. It is vital to define carefully the scope of such measures. Bringing too many or too few individuals within scope of measures like de-Ba'athification can have far-reaching consequences for public sector capacity and for the restoration of public trust in the institutions of government.

882. It is also important to think through the administrative implications of the measures to be applied and the process for their implementation.

883. The potential for abuse means that it is essential to have thought-through forms of oversight that are as impartial and non-partisan as possible.

Security Sector Reform

884. An SSR strategy should define the functions of different elements of the relevant security sector and the structures needed to perform those functions. Considering those questions should drive a robust debate about how security requirements might change over time.

885. An understanding of the many different models that exist internationally for internal security, policing and criminal justice is essential. But those models cannot be considered in isolation because what works in one country will not necessarily work in another which may have very different traditions. It is therefore critical for the SSR strategy to take full account of the history, culture and inherited practices of the country or region in question. The strategy also needs to be informed by the views and aspirations of the local population.

886. A strategy should set out the desired operating standard for each function and state how that differs, if at all, from what exists. In doing so, the strategy should specify where capacity needs to be developed and inform a serious assessment of how the material resources available could best be deployed.

887. It is essential that the UK has an appropriate way to measure the success of any SSR plan. If a clear strategy is in place and has taken account of the views of the local population, the indicators of that success should be obvious. It should rarely concentrate on a one-dimensional set of numbers but instead be a more qualitative and rounded assessment.

Resources

888. The direction in the Ministerial Code that the estimate of a cost of a proposal should be included in the memorandum submitted to Cabinet or a Ministerial Committee applies equally to military operations. When evaluating military options it is appropriate to consider financial risk alongside other forms of risk. While governments will rarely wish to preclude options solely on the basis of cost, they must also recognise that, over time, cost may become an issue and make it difficult to sustain a military operation over the longer term.

889. Strategies and plans must define the resources required to deliver objectives, identify the budget(s) that will provide those resources, and confirm that those resources are available.

890. In developing strategies and plans for civilian/military operations, a government should address the impact of the different mechanisms used to fund military operations and civilian activities and the extent to which those mechanisms provide perverse incentives for military action by making it easier to secure funding for agreed military operations than for civilian activities.

891. A government should also address its explicit and implicit financial policy that, while there should be no constraint on the provision of funding for military operations, it is reasonable that for the same civilian/military operation, departments should find funding for new civilian activities from within their existing budgets, which are likely to be fully allocated to existing departmental priorities.

892. A government is likely to embark on major civilian/military operations such as Iraq only rarely.

893. A government should recognise that, in such operations, the civilian components (including diplomatic activity, reconstruction and Security Sector Reform) will be critical for strategic success, may be very substantial, and must be properly resourced.

894. One arrangement would be to create a budget for the civilian components of the operation, under the direction of a senior Minister with lead responsibility and in support of a coherent UK strategy. Once allocations were made from that budget to individual departments, the allocations would be managed within departments' legal and policy constraints. Such an arrangement should:

- ensure that UK strategy was resourced;
- promote joint working;
- minimise the potential for gaming;
- be able to respond to in-year priorities; and
- reduce the amount of time that Ministers and senior officials need to spend arguing about funding individual activities.

895. The Inquiry recognises that, since 2003, significant changes have been made to the UK's strategic and operational approach to reconstruction and stabilisation, including to the arrangements for funding such operations.

Military equipment (post-conflict)

896. In deciding to undertake concurrent operations in Iraq and Afghanistan, the UK knowingly exceeded the Defence Planning Assumptions. All resources from that point onwards were going to be stretched. Any decision which commits the UK to extended operations in excess of the Defence Planning Assumptions should be based on the most rigorous analysis of its potential implications, including for the availability of relevant capabilities for UK forces.

897. At the start of Op TELIC, the MOD knew that it had capability gaps in relation to protected mobility and ISTAR and that either could have a significant impact on operations. Known gaps in such capabilities should always be clearly communicated to Ministers.

898. The MOD should be pro-active in seeking to understand and articulate new or additional equipment requirements. The MOD told the Inquiry that there was no simple

answer to the question of where the primary responsibility for identifying capability gaps lay during Op TELIC. That is unacceptable. The roles and responsibilities for identifying and articulating capability gaps in enduring operations must be clearly defined, communicated and understood by those concerned. It is possible that this has been addressed after the period covered by this Inquiry.

899. Those responsible for making decisions on the investment in military capabilities should continually evaluate whether the balance between current operational requirements and long-term defence programmes is right, particularly to meet an evolving threat on current operations.

900. During the first four years of Op TELIC, there was no clear statement of policy setting out the acceptable level of risk to UK forces and who was responsible for managing that risk. The MOD has suggested to the Inquiry that successive policies defining risk ownership and governance more clearly have addressed that absence, and that wider MOD risk management processes have also been revised. In any future operation the level of force protection required to meet the assessed threat needs to be addressed explicitly.

Civilian personnel

901. The Inquiry recognises that, since 2003, significant changes have been made to the UK's strategic and operational approach to reconstruction and stabilisation. Some of those changes, including the establishment of a deployable UK civilian stand-by capability, are the direct result of lessons learned from serious shortcomings in the deployment of civilian personnel in post-conflict Iraq.

902. The effectiveness of the UK civilian effort in post-conflict Iraq was compromised by a range of factors, including the absence of effective cross-government co-ordination on risk, duty of care and the terms and conditions applicable to personnel serving in Iraq.

903. The difficult working conditions for civilians in Iraq were reflected in short tour lengths and frequent leave breaks. Different departments adopted different arrangements throughout the Iraq campaign, leading to concerns about breaks in continuity, loss of momentum, lack of institutional memory and insufficient local knowledge.

904. Different departments will continue to deploy civilian staff in different roles. Standardisation of all aspects of those deployments may not be appropriate, but greater harmonisation of departmental policies should be considered wherever possible. The same approach should be applied to locally engaged (LE) staff.

905. At all stages, including planning, departments must give full consideration to their responsibilities and duty of care towards LE staff, who have an essential contribution to make and will face particular risks in insecure environments.

906. All civilian deployments should be assessed and reviewed against a single, rigorous, cross-government framework for risk management. The framework should provide the means for the Government as a whole to strike an effective balance between security and operational effectiveness, and to take timely decisions on the provision of appropriate security measures.

907. Standardising tour lengths for civilians deployed by different departments would have eased the overall administrative burden and, perhaps, some of the tensions between individuals from different government departments serving in Iraq. But the environment was difficult and individuals' resilience and circumstances varied. The introduction of the option to extend a tour of duty was an appropriate response.

908. Throughout any operation of this kind, departments should maintain two procedures for the systematic debriefing of staff returning to the UK: one to meet duty of care obligations, the other to learn lessons from their experience.

909. In order to identify individuals with the right skills, there must be clarity about the roles they are to perform. Wherever possible, individuals should be recruited for and deployed to clearly defined roles appropriate to their skills and seniority. They must be provided with the equipment needed to perform those roles to a high standard.

910. The Government should consider the introduction of a mechanism for responding to a surge in demand for a particular language capability.

911. The Inquiry views the inability of the FCO, the MOD and DFID to confirm how many civilian personnel were deployed to or employed in Iraq, in which locations and in what roles, as a serious failure. Data management systems must provide accurate information on the names, roles and locations of all staff for whom departments have duty of care responsibilities.

Timeline of events

Before 2001

2 August 1990	Saddam Hussein invades Kuwait
29 November 1990	Security Council adopts resolution 678
3 April 1991	Security Council adopts resolution 687
December 1998	Operation Desert Fox
2 June 1999	Ministerial Committee on Defence and Overseas Policy approves a policy of continuing containment
17 December 1999	Security Council adopts resolution 1284

2001

23 February	Mr Blair and President Bush agree on the need for a policy on Iraq which would be more widely supported in the Middle East
11 September	Al Qaida attacks the World Trade Center and the Pentagon
26 November	President Bush calls for weapons inspectors to return to Iraq

2002

29 January	President Bush makes his "axis of evil" speech
7 March	Cabinet discusses Iraq strategy
5-7 April	Mr Blair and President Bush meet in Crawford; Mr Blair makes his College Station speech
23 July	Mr Blair holds a meeting on Iraq policy
28 July	Mr Blair sends a Note to President Bush beginning "I will be with you, whatever"
6/7 September	Mr Blair and President Bush meet at Camp David
12 September	President Bush says he would put Iraqi non-compliance to the UN, paving the way for resolution 1441
24 September	Parliament recalled; dossier published
10/11 October	US Congress authorises use of force in Iraq
31 October	Decision to offer "Package 3" for planning purposes
8 November	Security Council adopts resolution 1441
13 November	Iraq announces it will comply with resolution 1441

2003

14 January	Lord Goldsmith gives his draft legal advice to Mr Blair
17 January	Decision in principle to deploy UK forces in southern Iraq
27 January	Dr Blix and Dr ElBaradei report to the Security Council
31 January	Mr Blair and President Bush meet in Washington
5 February	Secretary Powell's presentation to the Security Council
14 February	Dr Blix and Dr ElBaradei report to the Security Council

15 February	Stop the War protests held
24 February	UK/US/Spain table draft second resolution
7 March	Lord Goldsmith's advice on the legality of military action in Iraq; Dr Blix and Dr ElBaradei report to the Security Council
12 March	Recognition that the second resolution would not secure the support of a majority of the Security Council
13 March	Lord Goldsmith reaches his "better view" that invasion is legal
16 March	Azores Summit
17 March	Last Cabinet meeting before the invasion agrees Parliament should be asked to endorse the use of military action against Iraq
18 March	Parliamentary debate and vote on Iraq

Night of 19/20 March: invasion of Iraq begins

7 April	UK troops enter Basra
16 April	General Franks issues his "Freedom Message to the Iraqi People"
1 May	President Bush declares "Mission Accomplished"
16 May	Coalition Provisional Authority Order No.1 (de-Ba'athification of Iraqi Society)
22 May	Security Council adopts resolution 1483
23 May	Coalition Provisional Authority Order No.2 dissolves some Iraqi military and security structures
13 July	Inauguration of the Governing Council
19 August	Bomb attack on UN HQ at the Canal Hotel in Baghdad
23/24 October	Madrid Donors Conference
15 November	Timetable for creation of a transitional Iraqi administration announced
13 December	Capture of Saddam Hussein by US forces

2004

1 March	Transitional Administrative Law agreed
31 March	Ambush of four US security contractors sparks unrest in Fallujah
Late April	Photos of prisoner abuse at Abu Ghraib published
8 June	Security Council adopts resolution 1546
28 June	End of Occupation: inauguration of Iraqi Interim Government (Prime Minister Allawi)
29 June	Mr Blair announces HQ ARRC will deploy to Afghanistan

2005

30 January	Elections to the Transitional National Assembly
3 May	Iraqi Transitional Government takes power (Prime Minister Ja'afari)
21 July	Decision to deploy Provincial Reconstruction Team and military support to Helmand province, Afghanistan
15 October	Referendum on the Iraqi Constitution
19 October	US announces new "Clear-Hold-Build" strategy for Iraq
15 December	Parliamentary elections in Iraq

2006

26 January	Cabinet approves deployment to Helmand province
April to June	Formation of Maliki government
1 May	UK forces become responsible for Helmand
28 September	Op SINBAD begins in Basra
End October	Majority of UK civilian staff withdrawn from the Basra Palace site

2007

10 January	President Bush announces the US "surge"
27 June	Mr Blair leaves office; Mr Brown becomes Prime Minister
13 August	Start of reduction of Jaysh al-Mahdi violence against UK forces

| 2/3 September | UK forces leave the Basra Palace site |
| 16 December | Basra transitions to Provincial Iraqi Control |

2008

| 25 March | Start of Prime Minister Maliki's Charge of the Knights |
| 18 December | Mr Brown announces plans to withdraw the majority of UK troops |

2009 onwards

30 April 2009	Completion of the main UK military mission in Iraq
15 October 2009	UK/Iraq Training and Maritime Support Agreement ratified
22 May 2011	Departure of the last UK naval training team from Iraq